Finding

Abundant Life

in Jesus

Find out the **GREATEST DECISION** You Can Make

Discover the **7** Keys to Abundant Life

Follow God's Still Small Voice

With Small Group Bible Study Discussion Questions

By Ruel H. Castillo

Foreword by Dr. Paul E. Magnus

Edited and published by Aisha D. Hammah

WTL INTERNATIONAL

Finding Abundant Life in Jesus

Cataloguing data available from
Library and Archives Canada

Published by
WTL International
930 North Park Drive
P.O. Box 33049
Brampton, Ontario
L6S 6A7 Canada

www.wtlipublishing.com

ISBN 978-1-927865-07-1

Printed in the USA

10 9 8 7 6 5 4 3 2 1

All scriptures are from the New King James Version of the Holy
Bible unless otherwise noted.

Dedications

To my loving and perfect
Father God in heaven,

To my faithful and true
Lord and *Savior, Jesus Christ,*

To my constant teacher, helper and guide
God the *Holy Spirit*

To God be all the glory, honor and praise.

Table of Contents

Foreword

It was my pleasure meeting Ruel Castillo while serving as the Chair of Leadership at Tyndale Seminary. Ruel distinguished himself as an ardent student and a passionate follower of Jesus. It is with delight that I share a few reflective comments regarding his very first book, "*Finding Abundant Life in Jesus.*"

Ruel's high level of commitment and deep love for God alongside his intimacy with God become very evident as he provides 3 compelling reasons for us to read this book and then goes on to tell his life story and share 7 keys to abundant life. Ruel's life story of family rejection and abuse, his journey into unforgiveness and hatred, his unfulfilled ambitions, and his early relational problems have us wondering how his story will end.

To see the change in his life and attitudes when he gives his heart, mind, soul, and body over to God is encouraging as his journey changes completely when he makes the decision to follow Jesus. From being angry and challenging to live with, to becoming an amazing Christian lover, father, student and minister, his story is fine preparation for the reader to carefully consider his call toward moving from a life of pain and bitterness to an abundant life.

His challenge to us comes from a heart of experience and careful study of God and His word. The call for us to believe God, have faith in Him, love Him above all and unconditionally, obey Him wholeheartedly, fear Him, keep His commandments, focus on Him and trust in Him is perfectly suitable from a person who is so evidently far along on his journey of faith. My special congratulations and thanks go out to Ruel for sharing this, his first book, and to his wife, Jennifer, for allowing him the time to do so. The very best to you as you share and live the 7 keys to abundant life, Ruel.

Dr. Paul E. Magnus
President Emeritus and Distinguished Professor of Leadership/Management and Consultant/Coach/Facilitator, PJ Magnus Coaching & Consulting Ltd.

Introduction

*J*esus said that He has come that we might have life and have it more abundantly (John 10:10). Abundant life can only be found in surrendering our lives to the Lordship of Jesus Christ. He alone can give us eternal life and a victorious life on Earth.

There are **3 major reasons** why I believe you need to continue reading this book. Firstly, you are created by God and this book will help remove any doubts you might have of this important fact. Secondly, you are loved by God and this book will help draw a picture for you of the magnitude of this great love. Thirdly, you have a purpose in life and this book will help show you how to live in a manner in which you can fulfill that purpose.

If you wanted to know how to fly a jet, then you would study hard to get a license and seek proper training. The best training would come from the one who actually created the particular jet you were going to fly. You would certainly want to use the manual the manufacturer provided over any other. The same can be applied to learning how to get the best out of this journey called "life."

God created you, therefore the best way to live your life is by learning from Him and by following the manual for your life that was created by Him, which is the Bible. My book will help point you towards God the Father, God the Son, and God the Holy Spirit and His word. I will highlight many biblical scriptures that I hope will serve to align your path with God's will.

In this book, you will learn about the depth of the love God has for you. The Bible says, "For God so loved the world..." (John 3:16). It is important for you to understand the nature of His love for you. I will discuss this topic in the first part of my book.

I believe the best way to relate to you is to share the testimony of my life. My life story is in the second part of this book which features some of the miracles God has done throughout the course of my life.

I will also lay out what I have termed "7 Keys to Abundant Life." These are 7 ways to please the living God featured in the third part of this book. The Bible is a treasure book of keys or ways to please God so the 7 keys are drawn straight from Scripture.

The fourth part of this book outlines bonus topics and, finally, the fifth part of this book talks about the conclusion and the amazing miracle God did in my life.

I pray as you read each part of this book, God the Holy Spirit will speak to your heart in a special way so that you are encouraged to live a God-centered life.

The God Who Loves You

Jeremiah 31:3

"… I have loved you with an everlasting love; Therefore with lovingkindness I have drawn you."

*W*e live in a troubled world. Jesus said, "In the world you will have tribulation…" (John 16:33). Problems are real. Difficulties, hurt, pain, sorrow and trials are part of this life. The Bible tells us why. It is because the devil and his demons are here to steal, to kill and to destroy (John 10:10). God is not the source of your problems. God loves you and knows every detail of your life and He is willing to help you overcome all challenges you face if you will allow Him to work in your life.

This book brings good news to you because it declares that Jesus came so that you may have life and you may have it more abundantly. *Finding Abundant Life in Jesus is proof of this truth and following the 7 keys can help you to achieve the abundant life Jesus speaks of.*

Satan is the father of lies (John 8:44). He wants to deceive you and every other person on Earth (Revelation 12:9). Satan goes about like a roaring lion looking for someone to devour and will seize every opportunity to bring you down (1 Peter 5:8). Sin brings problem after problem in our lives. Sin, which is a transgression against God's law, brings difficulties, pain, sorrow and ultimately death.

I can say that I was once lost but now I am found. God did an amazing work in my life to get me to see the truth about Jesus, realize what Jesus did on the cross for me, and learn how I could have a relationship with a perfect and loving Father (Matthew 5:48). He used His voice, His word, believers and circumstances to help me understand the urgent need for me to receive Jesus as my Lord and Savior.

The greatest need of every person is not food, shelter or clothing but salvation through faith in the Lord Jesus Christ. The Bible says, "For the Son of Man has come to seek and to save that which was lost" (Luke 19:10).

The Parable of the Prodigal Son

God in His loving nature reaches out to us to initiate a relationship with Him. He finds great joy when we are reconciled to Him. A story in the Bible that I believe relates perfectly to each and every one of us is the Parable of the Prodigal Son which was told by Jesus.

[11] Then He said: "A certain man had two sons. [12] And the younger of them said to *his* father, 'Father, give me the portion of goods that falls *to me.*' So he divided to them *his* livelihood. [13] And not many days after, the younger son gathered all together, journeyed to a far country, and there wasted his possessions with prodigal living. [14] But when he had spent all, there arose a severe famine in that land, and he began to be in want. [15] Then he went and joined himself to a citizen of that country, and he sent him into his fields to feed swine. [16] And he would gladly have filled his stomach with the pods that the swine ate, and no one gave him *anything.*

[17] "But when he came to himself, he said, 'How many of my father's hired servants have bread enough and to spare, and I perish with hunger! [18] I will arise and go to my father, and will say to him, "Father, I have sinned against heaven and before you, [19] and I am no longer worthy to be called your son. Make me like one of your hired servants."'

[20] "And he arose and came to his father. But when he was still a great way off, **his father saw him and had compassion, and ran and fell on his neck and kissed him**. [21] And the son said to him, 'Father, I have sinned against heaven and in your sight, and am no longer worthy to be called your son.'

[22] "But the father said to his servants, 'Bring out the best robe and put *it* on him, and put a ring on his hand and sandals on *his* feet. [23] And bring the fatted calf here and kill *it,* and let us eat and be merry; [24] for this my son was dead and is alive again; he was lost and is found.' And they began to be merry." (Luke 15:11–24)

What happened to the prodigal son in the parable? He spent all of his inheritance and became needy. He suffered for some time from the consequences of his sins. He even worked feeding pigs. For the Israelites, the pig was one of the "unclean animals." After experiencing hunger, he envied the pigs, for no one gave him anything.

Verse 15 of the parable says that the prodigal son "joined himself to a citizen of that country." In times of difficulty, many people are looking for places or people to associate with. Many go to the wrong places and associate with the wrong people. The best way is to rest in the hands of the almighty Father in heaven. The Bible says we must, "Seek first the kingdom of God and His righteousness, and all these things shall be added to you" (Matthew 6:33).

The prodigal son knew enough to return to his father. He knew that his father was generous and merciful. He knew how kind his father was—that his father would hire him as a servant. *I want to tell you that you have a loving and forgiving Father in heaven waiting for you.* If you will seek Him with all your heart you will find Him (Deuteronomy 4:29).

In our story, the father upon seeing his lost son had compassion for him; so much that he ran towards him, wrapped his arms around him and kissed him. Clearly, the father was looking forward to seeing him come back home. It is important to notice that the son had not even completed speaking his words when the father had already extended him his complete forgiveness. The father gave him a robe, a ring and sandals as symbols of the restoration of the sonship. God rejoices the same way for each of us when we come to Him (Luke 15:6). **Always remember that God's love for you is greater than your sin**. He does not care how many sins we have committed or how many people we have hurt in the past. What He is after the most is our heart of full surrender to Him. The Scriptures tell us that "The Lord is near to the heartbroken and He saves those who are crushed in spirit (contrite in heart, truly sorry for their sin)" (Psalm 34:18 AMP).

God's compassion on Adam and Eve

Before God created Adam and Eve, He provided everything they would need. The garden that He placed them in was abundant in all the things they needed. Our evidence of this is the statement from Genesis, "Then God saw everything that He had made, and indeed *it* was very good" (Genesis 1:31). Adam and Eve lacked nothing. We have a God who wants to shower us with His blessings in life if we will follow His word and ways.

Adam and Eve disobeyed God through deception by Satan. (The account of the fall of Adam and Eve appears in Genesis 3.) The Bible tells us that after they sinned, God still provided tunics of skin to clothe the pair (Genesis 3:21). In this we can see God's love displayed.

God's loving plan of salvation

God made a plan to rescue man from his sins through the sacrifice of Jesus on the cross. Because of His just and holy nature, a sacrifice was needed. The perfect sacrifice was Jesus. The Bible declares, "… as Christ also has loved us and given Himself for us, an offering and a sacrifice to God for a sweet-smelling aroma" (Ephesians 5:2). Both the Father and the Son loved us before we were born on this earth.

God loves you

I want to assure you today that God loves you. God loves you no matter what you have done in the past. For the Bible tells us that, "…God demonstrates His own love toward us, in that while we were still sinners, Christ died for us" (Romans 5:8). He is a perfect Father (Matthew 5:48). There are fathers that love their children more than they love themselves. Imagine the love God has for us, Him being a perfect Father. God's motivation is love. One of the simplest definitions of Him is the well-known phrase, "God is love," which is a quote from 1 John 4:8.

The One who loves you most is God, the Creator of heaven and Earth. "For God so loved the world that He gave His only begotten Son, that whoever believes in Him should not perish but have everlasting life"

(John 3:16). Jesus died on the cross because of God's love for us. He endured the pain, torture and death needed to make a way for us to come home to our Father in heaven (1 Timothy 2:5–6).

God desires to give you the best and bring you to a place of abundance if you will allow Him to work in your life. I can guarantee you that your life will never be the same.

I have undergone deep pain, hurt and frustration but God showed me how to overcome all of this. Father God in heaven is waiting on your decision to come to Him through the sacrifice of His Son, Jesus Christ. He wants to restore your position as a child of God. He wants to bless you. Like the father in the Parable of the Prodigal Son, He is willing to forgive you from all your sins. He is able to heal your broken heart from all of your pain, hurt and frustration. Jesus said, "Come to Me, all *you* who labor and are heavy laden, and I will give you rest" (Matthew 11:28).

Similar to what the father of the prodigal son did, the Heavenly Father continuously looks for His children to come back home. Imagine how accurate and relevant this picture of God's love for you is—that God selected it to share in His word.

Another story of God's love for us is the Parable of the Lost Sheep found in Luke chapter 15. The same idea is communicated. The shepherd is willing to leave the 99 sheep that are accounted for to go after the one lost sheep. If you do not have Jesus as your Lord and Savior you are the lost sheep. Father God is waiting for your decision to return to Him through the sacrifice of His Son.

Do you want a gift from God? If you are willing, receive Jesus Christ today as your Lord and Savior, "For the wages of sin *is* death, but the gift of God *is* eternal life in Christ Jesus our Lord" (Romans 6:23).

Life Lessons:

- *The Parable of the Prodigal Son is a wonderful reminder that God is willing to forgive us and restore His relationship with us*

- *God loves us so much that He made a way to rescue us from the punishment of sin*

My Life Story and God's Miracles

My Early Years

$\mathcal{I}$t was in the Philippines where my father left when I was still in my mother's womb. My mother told me that she thought of aborting me because of what my father had done. This circumstance would have a great impact on my life.

My father never came back. He did not give financial support to my mother during my years growing up. Being a single parent, my mother worked very hard to meet our daily needs. Later on, my mother moved on and had more children.

Living without a father was very difficult and challenging for me. My mother and step father would argue almost every day. Due to a lack of finances, attending school became a daily challenge. The extent of my broken-heartedness was great. I lost hope in life until one day when my mother welcomed a pastor into our home to conduct a Bible study. I was curious about what the pastor and the people were doing in our home. They had Bibles and were praying, worshipping and studying with passion.

In my search for God, I soon attended a Christian worship service. At the end of the service, the Christians purposely gathered around me and asked if they could lead me in a *prayer of salvation*. I can still picture in my mind, the day they gathered around me as I prayed the prayer of salvation.

After the experience at the worship service, I began to realize a need to personally accept Jesus in my heart as my Lord and Savior. Even though I was regularly attending a Catholic Church, I did not understand this need to receive Jesus as the Lord and Savior of my life. **I decided to surrender my life to God.** In my bedroom, one day as a teenager, as I looked up at the clear blue sky, I cried out in tears to God to forgive me and help me. With all of my heart, I fervently asked Jesus to come into my heart and be my Lord and Savior repeatedly. I felt wonderful after that. I knew that something had happened in me that I cannot explain.

The search for my father

When I reached 18 years old, I decided to look for my father. My mother told me that my father was living in Tanauan, Batangas, Philippines and he had a daughter named Rowena.

I asked my classmate who was familiar with that city to join me in my search. After traveling for hours, we finally reached Tanauan, a place I had never visited before. We started asking questions to people around until we reached the Tanauan City Hall. When the mayor of the city heard my story, he was so touched by it that he gave us 50.00 pesos for our journey in search of my father. It was after the election and the mayor was kind enough to allow us to search the name of my father in the voter list for the city. We got 3 similar names sharing my father's first and last names, but they had different middle initials.

As we kept on asking for directions, we finally reached a house and as we knocked on the door, something unforgettable happened! The man who opened the door called me by my first name, "Ruel," and welcomed us into his home. Both my friend and I were surprised at the gesture. After talking to the family for some time, I learned that my father's firstborn to his first wife was also named "Ruel" and looked like me. As I told my story, they believed me and called other relatives to come see me. We went to see one of my aunts, who was a bank manager, and as we sat inside the boardroom of the bank, they were all staring at me.

They also showed us my grandparents' house. It was there I saw my father's image in a picture for the first time. I took my college picture and I held it closely beside my father's picture and I was surprised. He looked exactly like me. Nose, ears and face—they were all similar. In my heart, I told myself my search was over.

My father's relatives told me that my father was working in Quezon City Hall as an engineer. As we set off to find him, they gave us pocket money for our trip. My uncle, who was a Barangay Councilor, walked us up to the bus stop. We thanked every one of them and we departed from that place feeling joyful and loved.

I was excited about seeing my father, so the next day my classmate and I went to Quezon City Hall. As I entered the engineer's office, my heart was beating fast. This was the place of my father's employment. We asked for my father's desk, which we found after some time, and my classmate and I waited there. A man approached us and asked, "Who are you looking for?" I said we are looking for Reynaldo Castillo. He said, "I am Reynaldo Castillo." I said to him, "Do you remember Elena Hernandez (my mother's name)?" He answered, "Yes! Why?" I said, "I am Ruel Castillo." At this, he replied coldly, "Why are you using that name? I am not your father!" Those were the last words I heard from my father.

My heart was deeply hurt and broken but I believe through the help of the Lord, I was able to control myself and sadly left the office. This rejection from my father developed an even greater pain in my heart but an inner voice spoke to me and told me to **"be of good cheer,"** reminding me that I was already 18 years old and everything would be okay.

To fully understand my situation, I went to my father's first family. I saw my brothers and sisters for the first time. I was told that my father had left them too and he had another family. Their mother said to me, "I know your mother." Looking at me she said to her children, "This young man did not do anything wrong." If only it had been my father offering these kind words. I still remember that one of my sisters gave me a wooden cross necklace.

My stepfather

My stepfather and I did not have a good relationship. He was called the black sheep of his family. He made so many wrong choices as a youngster that he had not been able to finish school and we lived hand-to-mouth.

One time, my stepfather asked me to go to one of his sisters and tell a lie. He wanted me to say that my sister was in the hospital so that they would give us money for the hospital. I refused to do so and as a result, the house was filled with his abusive words. My heart was filled with anguish.

I received physical abuse from him. I once slept in a car because of the severity of the violence in the home. Over time, I developed a hatred for my stepfather. In my attempts to get away from him and the negativity of the home environment, I ran away once and decided to live in the streets, but my mother located me and brought me back home.

A bittersweet wedding day

Another difficult period in my life was when I got married. My mother did not attend my wedding. The main reason was that I was the breadwinner in the family and she had other plans for my life. But God orchestrated the perfect time for me to get married.

A Miraculous Cure

By April 14, 2004, there were a number of serious problems I was facing. I had the following issues related to heartbreak in my life:

1. Unforgiveness towards my father

2. Hatred towards my stepfather

3. Relationship problems with my mother

4. Financial difficulty (especially due to the economic crisis)

5. Frustration because of unfulfilled plans

6. Stress because of my stepfather. This was the most troubling issue I had. I had prayed for 10 years for my stepfather to change but he was still the same

I had so much on my mind and heart was deeply troubled that I constantly found myself asking God repeatedly:

"Are You there, Oh Lord?"

"Are You there, Oh Lord?"

"Are You there, Oh Lord?"

Then one day, while I was walking down the street, my legs started to hurt. I felt numbness from my feet going up my body. It got to the point that I could not walk. My wife's cousin named Sheila, who happened to be inside the *jeepney* (public transportation) when I entered, saw me struggling and helped me to arrive at the hospital.

Upon arriving at the hospital, I received emergency response. They laid me on a stretcher. At this point, I could not move any part of my body. I felt as if I were about to die. My "last words" were, "Lord, help me!" I was unconscious for some time.

When I woke up, I was in a hospital room. Inside my room were my wife, mother-in-law, aunt and a pastor friend. The doctors did everything they knew to help me but nothing seemed to be working. At times, I was so cold that I shivered. At other times, I was so hot that I shouted out. At one time I felt as if I was in hell. I believed it was the Lord who placed in my heart to look for a Bible. I asked my wife for a Bible and she found one in the lobby of the hospital. It was a Gideon's Bible.

The first time I read from the Bible out loud, I suddenly felt the temperature in my body stabilize, but when I closed the Bible and thought about my problems and pain in life, I got sick again. I read from the Bible again and felt better. The same thing happened the third time. Before this event, I did not believe the Bible completely.

Since I had doubts about the Bible, I decided I was going to read the Bible in 3 parts, the beginning, the middle and the end. Every time I read out loud, I would feel normal. My condition changed from extremely high fever to normal temperature, and from freezing, to normal again, every time I read the pages of the Bible. For 3 days, the doctors could not explain my case.

My first day at the hospital was April 14th, 2004. Three doctors worked on me and gave me the highest dose of medicine, a dose normally given to severe cases "50/50 patients." By the end of April 16th, the doctors had given up on me and decided to send me to another hospital. I started to think deeply about what was happening to me. I had constantly asked God for His presence and then this hospital experience happened where I was being healed only by reading the words of the Bible. I then made the decision to ask the doctors to please just send me home. The doctors met and agreed that this was something spiritual. They agreed to discharge me with a transfer letter for another hospital (a copy of this letter is included in the book). I also requested to have the Gideon's Bible, and they said, "Yes!"

At home what do you think I did? Of course, I did the only thing that healed my unexplainable condition. I read the Bible continuously while I observed to see whether my unknown illness would come back. It never did after days of reading the Bible. Because of the amount of liquid in my body from the medication I had taken, I often went to the bathroom. After a few days I recovered with a new passion and boldness.

Reading the Bible continuously made me realize the urgent need of my family to get saved from the punishment of sin through the sacrifice of Jesus on the cross. My first Bible study happened in our home with my mother, stepfather, brother and sisters. I taught them about the urgent need to receive Jesus as Lord and Savior. I believe it was April of 2004 when I held this first Bible study.

I want to share with you my hospital records from my 3-day miracle experience at RNN Doctors Hospital & Clinic in G.M.A., Cavite, Philippines:

PATIENT NAME:	ruel, castillo			HAMA			
DATE ADMITTED:	14/04/04			DATE DISCHARGED: 4/16/04		RM NO: 2	

OPEN 24 HRS.
EMERGENCY &
LYING-IN

✙ RNN DOCTORS HOSPITAL & CLINIC
"total commitment to quality patient care"

DATE	DESRIPTION	QTY	AMOUNT	DATE	DESCRIPTION	QTY	AMOUNT
	Admitting Fee		300.00				
	IV Line	3	1030.00				
	IV Fluid	4	1500.00				
	syringe	7	260.00				
	Ampule	9	2350.00				
	Vials	6	6000.00				
	Oral meds.	2	36.00				
	Laboratory	3	650.00				
	Room Use	2	750.00				
	02 inhalation		360.00				
Prof. Fee							
	DR DATU		1800.00				
	DR GEBANA		1000.00				
	DR ALCARDE		500.00				
	NURSING FEE		500.00				
	subtotal		17036.00				
Less:	Deposit		2500.00		disbented 10 % approved g ama		
TOTAL			14536.00				

Approved by:	DR. NUMER R. ALCARDE JR.	13,082.4	Prepared by: MS. MA. FARRA E. TURLA
	Chief Administrator		Technical Assistant

The hospital bill summary, amounting to17,036.00 pesos for the 3 days of confinement

The transfer letter from my doctor. The doctors
planned to transfer me to another hospital.
I requested to be sent home
with the Gideon's Bible instead

RNN DOCTORS INC.
MEDICAL & DIAGNOSTICS
Congressional Road, G.M.A., Cavite
Tel. No. (046) 890-05-62
TIN-340-661-788-VAT

OFFICIAL RECEIPT

Date 4-14-04

Received from Ruel Castillo
the sum of Pesos Two thousand five hundred pesos only
Corresponding as payment for:

A. Professional Fee:
B. Medical Services:
C. Meds/Miscellaneous:

downpayment upon confinement

Total Amount Due: ₱ 2,500.00

Verified Correct by:

Nº 1945   DR. R. DATU , M.D.

Clients Signature

50 Bklts (50x3) 0001-2,500
BIR Permit No. OCN 1AU000021892 • 11-19-2002
CD Social & Comm'l. Printers   Dasmarinas, Cavite

RNN DOCTORS INC.
MEDICAL & DIAGNOSTICS
Congressional Road, G.M.A., Cavite
Tel. No. (046) 890-05-62
TIN-340-661-788-VAT

OFFICIAL RECEIPT

Date 4/16/04

Received from Ruel, Castillo
the sum of Pesos 13 th eighty two
Corresponding as payment for:

A. Professional Fee:
B. Medical Services:
C. Meds/Miscellaneous:

fully paid by confinement

Total Amount Due: ₱ 13,082-00

Verified Correct by:

Nº 1953   Dr. Randy Dion , M.D.

Clients Signature

50 Bklts (50x3) 0001-2,500
BIR Permit No. OCN 1AU000021892 • 11-19-2002
CD Social & Comm'l. Printers   Dasmarinas, Cavite

The 2 official receipts from my hospital visit

After this miraculous cure, I began to realize the truthfulness of the Bible and that the Lord God had heard my cry and answered the question, **"Are you there, Oh Lord?"** God had answered my prayers with a miracle. When I asked the elder of our church what he thought had happened to me, he said, **"God will use you."**

God continues to do His work in me

Following the miracle involving the hospital, I became a passionate follower of Jesus Christ. I began to love praying and reading the word of God, and started seeking Him more and more. However, even though I served and loved God, I still had a number of problems. I had unforgiveness, hatred, hurt about unfulfilled ambitions and a very strained relationship with my mother.

Living with my heart in this condition made me a very difficult person to deal with. I was overly sensitive and got angry very easily. People that I loved were often hurt by my words without me knowing it.

I remember praying for the Lord to make me a good husband, a good father and a faithful servant. I started to ask that He send people along my path to help me overcome myself. The Lord answered this prayer also. He sent pastors, teachers and godly friends who were instrumental in shaping my life with Him. The greatest Helper I received was God the Holy Spirit.

When I attended my first spiritual encounter (a Christ-centered retreat for growth and development) at Windsor Christian Fellowship in Ontario, Canada, God revealed to me that there was a lot of unforgiveness in my heart. The Lord revealed to me that I needed to forgive my stepfather. As I obeyed the Lord and shared the word of God with my stepfather and my mother, I saw them in a whole new way. I realized that they were also victims of abuse in their pasts. They also experienced pain and suffering. They, too, needed the Lord in order to be healed.

Through God's help, our relationship was eventually healed. As the love of God grew inside of me, I began to love others better and I forgave my parents.

As I continued to read and meditate on the word of God, I could see the Scriptures being fulfilled right before my eyes. I could see the truth about my situation. I began to love others unconditionally. I was able to shower my love on my wife, daughter and son. I was able to teach my family God's way.

Miracles in My Life

*N*ow, I am aware that the Lord has kept me safe and always given me "open doors" in life, sometimes literally! For example, as a young student, many times I could not study at home. My mother and stepfather would argue and shout at each other and this was very distracting. The Lord gave me neighbors that would open their doors for me to study. Many times they gave me food to eat.

At one time, I remember very clearly, my stepfather got upset when my mother gave me money for my studies. Because of this, I sometimes had to ask for money from the neighbors and my relatives just to be able to go to school. This was how my studies were sometimes supported.

As another example, the Lord opened the way for me to study in college by providing work as a part-time waiter at The Manila Hotel. This was a 5-star hotel located in Rizal Park. I was underage and had no experience at all but the Lord miraculously opened the door for me and I was offered work.

God also helped me vocationally. He provided me with a Ramon Magsaysay Junior Scholarship Grant and I was approved for a "Study Now—Pay Later" program. He also moved the heart of our University's Vice President to pay for my tuition. He helped me to believe I could become an engineer and I did become a licensed civil engineer as well as a licensed real estate broker.

Even though God was there all along the way opening doors for me, there is a collection of distinct and very unforgettable miracles that I want to share for the remainder of this section.

1. God helped me when a firecracker was blown in my face

There have been numerous serious injuries and even deaths on record that were a result of using firecrackers during the New Year celebrations in the Philippines. I am one on the list of those injured. When I was a child in Manila, I had a five-star firecracker accidentally explode in my face. I was rushed to the hospital. I could not see properly and my face was in bandages for weeks. I thought that my face would be completely disfigured by the accident. I was sure my eardrums had been damaged by the intensity of the sound. But by God's grace, I was healed from all complications.

2. God intervened on a roller-coaster ride

Also once when I was a child, I was on a well-known roller-coaster ride in the Philippines one day when harm presented itself. While standing on the roller coaster, my leg slipped and got caught on the running steel chains. I could feel the tightening of the steel chains reaching my leg bone. What great pain I felt! But a miracle happened that day. Suddenly, the roller coaster stopped and then slowly ran in the reverse direction which enabled my leg to be freed instead of being crushed. I looked around and I did not see anyone operating the ride. I believe it was God who saw me helpless. He saved my leg from being crushed by the running chains of the roller coaster.

3. God rescued me from the falling branch of a huge tree

While I was in high school one afternoon, my friend, Rovic Rosete, and I were walking towards our school after a break when a dead branch of a huge tree fell one step behind us. We were only one step away from being hit on our heads by the huge branch. I believe God prevented the dead branch from falling on top of our heads and possibly causing us severe injury or even killing us.

4. God rescued me in Saudi Arabia

I worked in Saudi Arabia where others said I received my second life. I suffered a serious car accident while I was on the way to work one day in a heavy sandstorm in the desert. The car I was in tumbled 3 times but, again, by God's grace, I made it out alive and I was healed from all injuries.

5. God extended the life of my mother

On a Thursday afternoon in August of 2008, while I was at our company training in Brampton, Ontario, Canada, the presence of the Lord came strongly where I was. I could sense the Lord walking towards me. It was around 3:00 p.m. I could feel the Lord urging me to pray for my mother. While in the middle of the training, I closed my eyes and started praying. I prayed for half an hour without others noticing me.

After praying hard for my mother, the strong presence of God left me and I began to be able to listen to the trainer again. I believe the Lord covered me so that others did not know I had been praying. At the end of the training, we had a summary closing game. I remember I could not participate properly because my mind was on my mother.

Then on Saturday of that week I called back home to the Philippines. My mother told me that she had lost consciousness and collapsed on the floor. She had been rushed to the hospital due to heart complications. The findings were an enlargement of the heart and high blood pressure. The doctors feared my mother would suffer a stroke.

My mother thought that it was her time to die. She told me that she had been thinking about me. She was thinking to herself, *My son is in Canada and he doesn't know I'm here dying.*

Miraculously, while my mother was lying on the hospital bed in Romblon, Philippines, I was praying for her through God's intervention in Ontario. In the hospital, my mother was unconscious but she eventually was able to open her eyes. She remembered seeing a thermos and then she felt the strength to sit up. My sister, who was looking after her, was surprised that she was able to sit up. She later stood up and eventually was able to walk out of the hospital on her own two feet.

The Lord healed my mother. After hearing the details about how I came to pray for her that day at the company training session, my mother's words to me were, **"The Lord extended my life. Now I don't have any pain in my body."**

Upon writing this book it has been 7 years and my mother is still alive and thanking God for the miracle He did in her life.

6. **God blessed me with His miraculous touch**

As I obeyed God in being a follower of Jesus, I encountered much opposition. I was experiencing difficulty after difficulty to the point where my heart was deeply troubled. In September of 2007, I was kneeling in prayer on the rooftop of a building in Brampton one day. I was in tears as I asked God to reveal Himself to me. As I persisted, suddenly I felt the Lord touch my face. I could sense that He came from above towards me, touched my face and then withdrew above. *I felt God's presence and a heavenly feeling when this happened and there was an unexplainable feeling of joy, peace and love.* It could not have been of this earth. In response, I was so joyful that whole week. In my heart, the verse from Romans 8:18 came to me, "I consider that our present sufferings are not worth comparing with the glory that will be revealed in us" (NIV).

I took 12 stones from that place where God touched me. I placed them in a glass container.

A picture of the Hospital's Gideon Bible and the 12 stones in a glass container on display in our living room as a memorial of the miracles God did in my life

The Greatest Decision

*T*he greatest decision I made is when I received Jesus to be my Lord and Savior. I believe with all my heart that it is the greatest decision every person on the planet needs to make. If you have not received Jesus Christ, it is very important that you do so. What does the Bible teach about Jesus? Here are scriptures that speak of Him.

> "For the wages of sin is death, but the gift of God is eternal life in Christ Jesus our Lord." (Romans 6:2)

> "For there is born to you this day in the city of David a Savior, who is Christ the Lord." (Luke 2:11)

> "For God so loved the world that He gave His only begotten Son, that whoever believes in Him should not perish but have everlasting life." (John 3:16)

> "...That if you confess with your mouth the Lord Jesus and believe in your heart that God has raised Him from the dead, you will be saved." (Romans 10:9)

From these verses we can conclude that Jesus is Lord and Savior.

Eternal life is a GIFT from our Father in heaven.

Do you want a gift that will change your life forever?

Do you want to experience His miracles in your life?

Do you want the best in your life?

Do you want the best for your family?

Do you want the greatest Friend in the world?

Do you want Someone to help you in every area of need?

There's an opportunity for you. DON'T MISS IT!

If you have not received Jesus Christ as your Lord and Savior, *"Behold, now is the accepted time; behold, now is the day of salvation"* (2 Corinthians 6:2).

I invite you to pray these words with all your heart and make this prayer your own:

Lord Jesus, forgive me of my sins.

Come into my heart.

I believe you died on the cross and rose again.

I receive you as my Lord and Savior.

Fill me with Your Spirit.

In your name, I pray. Amen.

When you received Jesus as your Lord and Savior, you become a child of a loving and perfect Father in heaven. Ask the Lord for a Christian Church for you to attend. I encourage you to always pray and read your Bible. God will answer our prayers in His perfect timing and according to His will.

Be faithful to our Lord Jesus Christ. It is my prayer that you will be successful and prosperous in life as you love God and obey Him in all areas.

Life Lessons:

- *Our God is a God of miracles*

- *When you align yourself with God, you can experience His powerful hand at work in your life*

- *With God all things are possible*

Part III

7 Keys

to Abundant Life

*L*ord **Jesus** said, "…I have come that they may have life, and that they may have it more abundantly" (John 10:10). Abundant life can only be found in surrendering our lives to the Lordship of Jesus Christ. He alone can give us eternal life and a true victorious life on earth.

From the time my father left us to where the Lord God has brought me to today, I can testify that the Lord Jesus has given me a taste of "abundant life." It is not to say that He is finished with me. I know that He will continue to complete what He has started with me, as Philippians 1:6 promises, "…He who has begun a good work in you will complete it until the day of Jesus Christ. I believe that there is more to come in my service to God. I feel safe and secure because I know He is a Good Shepherd and a Perfect Father.

In this segment, I am going to show you 7 concrete and proven ways that you can live your life, I named these "*7 Keys to Abundant Life*" because I believe if you will carefully follow them with all of your heart, they will bring you to an abundant life in Jesus. Problems will come but you are an overcomer with the Spirit of Jesus.

There is no other way to heaven but Jesus (John 14:6). There is no steadier foundation in life than God's word. There is no better plan for your life than God's plan (Jeremiah 29:11). But you have to do your part to set these into action. I pray that this section will guide, teach, encourage and equip you to do this. These keys are applicable no matter what your present situation in life is. I have found that they prove themselves to be true all of the time.

The 7 Keys to Abundant Life are as follows:

1. *Believe God Above All*
2. *Have Faith in God*
3. *Love God Above All and Unconditionally*
4. *Obey God Above All*
5. *Fear God Above All*
6. *Keep God's Commandments*
7. *Focus on God and Trust in Him*

KEY 1

Believe God Above All

Romans 4:3

"For what does the Scripture say? 'Abraham believed God, and it was accounted to him for righteousness.'"

$\mathcal{T}$o live the abundant life God has for us we must believe Him (The Creator) above any created being (man or woman). **Always remember that with God all things are possible.** We must believe God despite the discouraging circumstances we see around us, like Abraham who did not consider his own body or his wife's body but he considered His God who promised (Romans 4:19). We must believe God's word and His still small voice (1 Kings 19:12) above any teaching or human experience. This means that when there is a difference in what God says compared to what we see or hear, we must make a firm decision *to believe only what God says in His word or His still small voice.*

Reasons why we must believe God above all

1. **He alone is God**

   Our God is one God in 3 persons—God the Father, God the Son, and God the Holy Spirit— yet He is one (1 John 5:7). In Isaiah 43:10-11, God says of Himself, "Before Me there was no God formed, nor shall there be after Me. I, even **I, am the Lord, and besides Me there is no Savior.**" We must believe God above all because there is no one else besides Him who knows everything.

2. **He is the supreme ruler forever**

   God rules by His power forever. He created all things in existence (Genesis 1:1). He owns all things (Psalm 24:1). God is supreme over all other beings, principalities and powers, and His reign is not limited by time (Ephesians 1:21).

These are the words of King Nebuchadnezzar describing his personal witness to the wonder and supremacy of God. *"How great are His signs, and how mighty His wonders! His kingdom is an everlasting kingdom, and His dominion is from generation to generation"* (Daniel 4:3). Psalm 102:27 highlights the unchanging nature of God and the everlasting quality of this nature. It says, "...but You *are* the same, and Your years will have no end." Psalm 66:7 says, "He rules by His power forever." We can be sure God rules now and will rule forever. His kingdom will never end.

Every prideful leader in history—as told in the Bible—God is able to put down. Scripture tells us, "And those who walk in pride He is able to put down" (Daniel 4:37). The truth is "...The Most High rules in the kingdom of men, and gives it to whomever He chooses" (Daniel 4:25).

3. For Him 1000 years is like yesterday

God is eternal. God's scale is grand. In Psalm 90:4 it declares, "For a thousand years in Your sight are like yesterday when it is past, and *like* a watch in the night. In 2 Peter 3:8 it says, "But, beloved, do not forget this one thing, that with the Lord one day is as a thousand years, and a thousand years as one day." To God, a thousand years are just like one passing day. They are as brief as a few night hours. We can be sure our problems are not too big for Him. Though they might seem like mountains to us, they are small matters to Him.

4. All things are possible with Him

Even the sun once stood still and the moon stopped its course at God's command (Joshua 10:12). Therefore, we can be sure that when God declares something about our lives or makes a promise, He is able to make it happen. God is capable of making even what seems impossible happen.

Below are some of Lord Jesus' miracles:

1. He commanded a storm to be still (Matthew 8)

2. He called a man from the grave after 4 days of being dead (John 11)

3. He fed five 5000 people with 5 loaves and 2 fish. After that 12 basketfuls of bread and fish were collected (Matthew 14)

4. He turned water into wine (John 2)

5. He walked on the sea (Matthew 14)

6. He healed 2 blind men (Matthew 20)

7. He cast out demons (Mathew 8–9)

As Creator, God can do anything. You can search the Bible—it is full of miracles.

5. He limits the power of Satan (our enemy)

The Bible says, "God is faithful, who will not allow you to be tempted beyond what you are able, but with the temptation will also make the way of escape, that you may be able to bear it" (1 Corinthians 10:13). In Job 1 and 2, God completely controls the situation Job finds himself in. If God is in control of everything, we have to understand that He knows the challenges we are facing and that with Him there is restoration. *He alone knows the perfect way out of your problems.* The best way for us is to come to Him and ask for His help and guidance in every situation. *To ask Him before every decision is the wisest way to live life on earth* (Proverbs 3:6).

Abraham believed God

In Genesis, Abraham obeyed God's voice (Genesis 12:4) in leaving his family and country. In Genesis 15:13–15, God speaks of the future concerning Abraham and his descendants.

> [13] Then He said to Abram: "Know certainly that your descendants will be strangers in a land *that is* not theirs, and will serve them, and they will afflict them four hundred years. [14] And also the nation whom they serve I will judge; afterward they shall come out with great possessions. [15] Now as for you, you shall go to your fathers in peace; you shall be buried at a good old age.

At the time God spoke these words, Abraham had no child. No one could see any evidence that God's promise would come true. Abraham's and Sarah's bodies were both as good as dead as far as child bearing was concerned. *We should follow the example of Abraham who chose to believe God even though he faced a very discouraging reality.*

Good traits of Abraham

1. Abraham believed the Lord when He spoke to him about his future (Genesis 15:6).

2. Abraham did not waver in believing the promise of God but was strong in his faith (Romans 4:20).

3. Abraham was fully convinced that God was able to perform what He had promised (Romans 4:21).

4. Abraham obeyed the voice of God and chose actions to follow through with his faith (Genesis 12).

35

God revealed future events that happened exactly as promised

God is eternal and all powerful. He is so awesome that He can declare the outcome of an event far before it happens. Isaiah 46:10 describes Him as, "Declaring the end from the beginning,

And from ancient times *things* that are not *yet* done." *God speaks of things to happen in the future and lays out His plans before mere men.* There are many examples of this in the Bible. Here are a few from the lifetime of Abraham:

1. Roughly 200 years before the time of Israel's 400 years of bondage in Egypt, God declared to Abraham in Genesis 15:13, "Know certainly that your descendants will be strangers in a land *that is* not theirs, and will serve them, and they will afflict them four hundred years." God even revealed how long the time of affliction and it happened exactly as God spoke it.

> The greatest power in the universe I believe is the spoken words of God (Psalm 33:9). Our responsibility is to believe it and receive it with all our heart and mind.

2. God declared that the Israelites would come out of their land of bondage with great possessions (Genesis 15:14) around 600 years before it actually did happen. Exodus 12:36 records that when the Israelites came out of Egypt, they were given whatever they requested from their former masters to take with them. The verse says that the Israelites "plundered" the Egyptians when they left.

3. God declared that Abraham would be buried at a good old age more than 90 years before it

happened. Genesis 25 tells us that Abraham died at the age of 175 years.

When God says that something will happen, we can be sure it will happen. His word does not fail. His word reminds us of this as it says:

> "So shall My word be that goes forth from My mouth; It shall not return to Me void, But it shall accomplish what I please, And it shall prosper *in the thing* for which I sent it." (Isaiah 55:11)

In Psalm 89:34, God says, "My covenant I will not break, Nor alter the word that has gone out of My lips." God knows what will happen and He has the power to make it happen. We can believe God because of this and because all of the things He said will happen up to this date have happened. He is a God who cannot lie.

What God says about you

So what does God say about you? Proverbs 23:18 of the New International Version of the Bible states that for those who are zealous for the fear of the Lord, "There is surely a future hope for you, and your hope will not be cut off." God also promises that if you delight in Him, He will "give you the desires of your heart." This encouraging promise is found in Psalm 37:4.

Life Lessons:

- *God wants our belief and faith in Him so that He can perform great things in our lives*

- *God knows the future things to come and has power over all things*

- *God rewards our belief in Him*

- *God says good things about those who choose to believe in Him*

Bible Study Discussion Questions:

1. As explained, what are the reasons why we must believe God and His word above all?

2. What do you admire in Abraham's walk with God?

3. What can you say about the power of God to declare future things to happen?

4. What do you think are the reasons why some people doubt or do not believe the God of the Bible?

5. Why do you think we need courage to believe God in this generation?

6. In the Bible, can you name a person or people who believed God and what happened? In contrast, name a person or people who do not believe God and what happened?

7. Have you experienced standing for your belief in God? Share your story.

8. Based on the lesson and discussion, what can we apply in our daily life?

KEY 2

Have Faith in God

$\mathcal{F}$aith in God is important because without faith we cannot please God. Even if we have other godly traits but have no faith, we cannot please God. It is through faith we please God. The Bible tells us, "...Without faith *it is* impossible to please *Him,* for he who comes to God must believe that He is, and *that* He is a rewarder of those who diligently seek Him" (Hebrews 11:6).

The Bible defines faith in Hebrews 11:1 by saying, "Now faith is the substance of things hoped for, the evidence of things not seen." In other words, faith is the confidence that what we hope for will actually happen. It is assurance of things we cannot see. Faith in God means we believe God, we believe who the Bible says He is and we are confident that He will do whatever He has promised. Others define faith as a strong belief in God.

The Bible tells us how we can have faith. "...Faith comes by hearing, and hearing by the word of God" (Romans 10:17). Knowing the Bible well is the source of a strong believer's faith.

God said to Joshua:

> "This Book of the Law shall not depart from your mouth, but you shall meditate in it day and night, that you may observe to do according to all that is written in it. For then you will make your way prosperous, and then you will have good success." (Joshua 1:8)

If God expects this of Joshua, it means He expects this of us. Just as He promises Joshua, continuously studying the word of God and applying it in your life will bring you success and prosperity.

Great faith

It is amazing what having faith in God can accomplish in this life. Let us examine a Bible passage that tells of a woman who had great faith in God.

> [21] Then Jesus went out from there and departed to the region of Tyre and Sidon. [22] And behold, a woman of Canaan came from that region and cried out to Him, saying, "Have mercy on me, O Lord, Son of David! My daughter is severely demon-possessed."

[23] But He answered her not a word.

And His disciples came and urged Him, saying, "Send her away, for she cries out after us."

[24] But He answered and said, "I was not sent except to the lost sheep of the house of Israel."

[25] Then she came and worshiped Him, saying, "Lord, help me!"

[26] But He answered and said, "It is not good to take the children's bread and throw *it* to the little dogs."

[27] And she said, "Yes, Lord, yet even the little dogs eat the crumbs which fall from their masters' table."

[28] Then Jesus answered and said to her, "O woman, great *is* your faith! Let it be to you as you desire." And her daughter was healed from that very hour. (Matthew 15:21–28)

By the last verse in this passage, Jesus commends the gentile woman with the words, "O woman, great is your faith! Let it be to you as you desire." Because of faith in God, the woman was commended by Jesus. Furthermore, she received the miracle she sought. She was blessed because of her great faith. She had faith in Jesus that He could heal her daughter. Although she could not understand how this would take place, she did not doubt that He could do it.

Jesus heals a centurion's servant

Let us examine a second passage.

[5] Now when Jesus had entered Capernaum, a centurion came to Him, pleading with Him, [6] saying, "Lord, my servant is lying at home paralyzed, dreadfully tormented."

[7] And Jesus said to him, "I will come and heal him."

[8] The centurion answered and said, "Lord, I am not worthy that You should come under my roof. But only

speak a word, and my servant will be healed. [9] For I also am a man under authority, having soldiers under me. And I say to this *one,* 'Go,' and he goes; and to another, 'Come,' and he comes; and to my servant, 'Do this,' and he does *it.*"

[10] When Jesus heard *it,* He marveled, and said to those who followed, "Assuredly, I say to you**, I have not found such great faith**, not even in Israel! [11] And I say to you that many will come from east and west, and sit down with Abraham, Isaac, and Jacob in the kingdom of heaven. [12] But the sons of the kingdom will be cast out into outer darkness. There will be weeping and gnashing of teeth." [13] Then Jesus said to the centurion, "Go your way; and **as you have believed, *so* let it be done for you.**" And his servant was healed that same hour. (Matthew 8:5–13)

In this passage, the centurion received his miracle because of his great faith. He came to Jesus believing that He was able to heal his servant and he believed in the power and authority of Jesus' word to heal.

Faith is rewarded

Both the woman and the centurion in the passages were considered by Jesus as having great faith. They both possessed a strong belief in the power, love and compassion of God. They both believed that Jesus is the healer. Both received the miracles of healing they asked for.

Let us also remember that because of faith, Abraham received a child from his wife who was well past her child-bearing years and Noah's family was chosen from all of the earth to be saved from destruction by the Great Flood.

Remarkable things can happen by having faith. I encourage you to have faith in God and His ability to meet your needs whatever they are.

Faith in God's still small voice

Our walk with God is amazing. During my hospital miracle as I shared in Part II of this book, God healed me through my reading of the Bible in the hospital. Now, God is showing me that He can speak to me by His Spirit living inside of me.

Below are scriptures that explain that a believer is the temple of the Holy Spirit.

- Do you not know that you are the **temple** of **God** and *that* the Spirit of **God** dwells in you (1 Corinthians 3:16)?

- Or do you not know that your body is the **temple** of the Holy Spirit *who is* in you, whom you have from **God**, and you are not your own (1 Corinthians 6:19)?

How wonderful was the sacrifice of Lord Jesus on the cross that the Holy God can dwell in me and in every believer! Everywhere I go, the Holy Spirit is there because I am God's temple. We must believe in Lord Jesus' promises below:

- "I will not leave you orphans; I will come to you." (John 14:18)

- "…I am with you always, even to the end of the age. Amen." (Matthew 28:20)

- "…Nevertheless I tell you the truth. It is to your advantage that I go away; for if I do not go away, the Helper will not come to you; but if I depart, I will send Him to you." (John 16:7)

- "…However, when He, the Spirit of truth has come, He will guide you into all truth; for He will not speak on His own authority, but whatever He hears He will speak; and He will tell you things to come." (John 16:13)

It is clear that Lord Jesus spoke of the coming of the Holy Spirit Who would be a Helper to every believer. According to Lord

Jesus, God the Holy Spirit would guide us into all truth. Scripture tells us that there is no unrighteousness in Him and it is impossible for God to lie, so we can count on His promises about the Holy Spirit.

As I meditate on the Scripture about the Holy Spirit, especially the words "...**the sheep hear His voice**..." (John 10:3). My faith is that God my Father in heaven is a perfect Father, my Lord Jesus Christ is the Good Shepherd and God the Holy Spirit is my constant Helper. My faith is that God will take care of my life and family as I obey Him and His blessing will overtake me.

My wife and I prayed and agreed together for a son and the Lord granted it. My wife became pregnant and the doctor said that since Jennifer had already had 2 Caesarian sections (C-sections), she would require a C-section on the delivery of our third baby." We both agreed on that decision.

God's still small voice in our lives

Our home is open one day a week for small group Bible study meetings. Once during a meeting, while were in worship and prayer time, the Lord spoke to my spirit the words, "It is normal." Upon hearing it the first time, I did not consider it fully. But again, God the Holy Spirit spoke to me during the small group worship: "It is normal." Upon hearing this the second time, I started to search the Scriptures and found Deuteronomy 28:2: "And all these blessings shall come upon you and overtake you, because you obey the voice of the Lord your God." I found many promised blessings to the people who obeyed God's voice in the Bible. I learned that Abraham was willing to offer Isaac as sacrifice in obedience to God's voice (Genesis 22). God blessed Abraham greatly because of his obedience. Noah obeyed God's voice and then his family members were saved from the Great Flood (Genesis 6). Philip obeyed God's voice and the Ethiopian eunuch possessing great authority was saved (Acts 8). Apostle Peter obeyed God's voice and Cornelius, with his household, was filled with the Holy Spirit and was baptized with water (Acts 10). Apostle Paul believed the voice of the Lord (Acts 23:11) despite difficult challenges and then God fulfilled His spoken word (Acts 28).

God confirmed His voice

So, I decided in my heart to follow His still small voice with a condition if I should hear it the third time. As I waited patiently during our small group worship time the Lord spoke again: "It is normal." Upon hearing this the third time I was fully convinced that this is from God. I began to pray that I will be obedient to His voice. I started to talk to my wife and explain that God was telling me something. It was not easy for her to say "yes" to me because of her respect for the doctor. So I continued to pray for wisdom and guidance. God gave me wisdom to explain to the doctor that if my son would be in the right position for normal delivery that I being the father would consider NORMAL birth for my son. The doctor coldly responded to me, "I WILL NOT SUPPORT YOU."

What should I do now? The doctor would not consider my suggestion that came from God the Holy Spirit. The Scripture tells us that Abraham did not consider his body but considered His God. **I DECIDED TO BELIEVE GOD EVEN THOUGH I WAS NOT SUPPORTED BY THE DOCTOR.**

As I continued to believe, my wife started to believe in me as well. Then, God sent good Christian friends to help us in different ways. I noticed God's power at work as I continued to believe. Weeks passed by…then months. On the day of the ultrasound, I rejoiced loudly when our baby was in the right position for normal delivery. For me, this was God's work aligning things to fulfill His words spoken to me.

On the day of the delivery, my wife was screaming in pain during contractions. Another doctor talked to me, discouraging me. The doctor told me to give up the plan for a normal delivery. A nurse would come by and say discouraging words as well, questioning why I was holding on to the idea of a normal delivery. I kept quiet knowing that they all wanted me to give up. I chose to hold on to believing in God's still small voice that said, "It is normal."

Praying, confessing and declaring God's word

I decided to close the room after everybody else left and then I began to pray, confess and declare God's word out loud with all my heart.

- You are God who will not fail us

- With God all things are possible

- Not a word will fail which the Lord God has spoken

- Your word will never come back void

- Your word is forever settled in heaven

- You are forever faithful and true

- You are our CREATOR and nothing is too hard for you

While praying and confessing these words out loud in the hospital room (in October 2012), suddenly God sent another nurse—a Christian. After some time, our baby came out safely by a NORMAL delivery. We received from the Lord "a healthy baby boy." We exceedingly rejoiced together and thanked God for His guidance and strength.

I discovered that God is

true and faithful

to His still small voice.

After few days, my wife fully recovered and said, "I thank God that I obeyed my husband." She was thankful because she did not undergo the painful C-section surgery. I was also thankful that I could hug her without her complaining of the wounds on her belly caused by C-section surgery. Her previous 2 C-sections had caused her to have pain for months and even years.

I named our son "SAMUEL JOHN." Why Samuel? As I remember early in life as a kid growing up in a difficult environment, I heard someone speaking to me. If found that if I followed His voice I had success, but when I disobeyed I had troubles. My question when I was a kid was, *Who is this speaking to me?* Many years passed by until I learned that it was the Lord Holy Spirit who was speaking to me to help me. I can relate myself to Prophet Samuel with his experience in hearing God's voice (1 Samuel 3).

In addition, it is because I obeyed God's still small voice. Like Prophet Samuel who obeyed God's voice (1 Samuel 16). Prophet Samuel anointed David upon hearing the voice of God. He could not see the physical appearance in considering the suitability for David as king but Prophet Samuel chose obedience to God's voice.

Life Lessons:

- *Without faith it is impossible to please God*
- *We should meditate on the word of God constantly to grow in our faith*
- *Remarkable things can happen through your faith in God's word and His still small voice*

Bible Study Discussion Questions:

1. According to the lesson, how can we develop our faith?
2. Define faith in your own words?
3. In the story in Matthew 15:21–28, what can you say about the woman's persistence?
4. In the story in Matthew 8:5–13, what can you say about the centurion's faith?
5. Can you name a person or people who had faith God in the Bible and what was the result of their faith in God? In contrast, can you name a person or people who have no faith in God and what happened?

6. In this sinful generation, how can we CONSTANTLY keep our faith in God despite negative situations, oppositions and attacks from the enemy?

7. Read the heroes of faith in Hebrews 11. Who do you admire the most and why?

8. Based on the lesson and discussion, what can we apply in our daily life?

KEY 3

Love God Above All and Unconditionally

*W*hy is it important to love God above all? How can you love God unconditionally? Loving God above all is the most important of the 7 keys. Lord Jesus said, *"You shall love the Lord your God with all your heart, with all your soul, and with all your mind."* This is referred to as the first and great commandment" (Matthew 22:37). Lord Jesus tells us plainly that this is the most important thing we can do. If you want to have the abundant life Jesus died for, you must set your heart on loving God above any created being or anything else.

Ways to love God unconditionally

How can we love God unconditionally? Unconditionally means without condition or limitation. Our problems in life are the reason why at times we question the love of God. Below are ways you can approach life that will cause you to love God unconditionally despite problems.

1. **Accept that problems are part of life**

    Part of loving God unconditionally is accepting that problems are a part of life. This does not mean to accept that the problems will bring us down. We are to have faith in the fact that God can bring us through our problems and He has the solutions. However, we are to be aware that we will face problems for certain. Jesus says, "...In the world you will have tribulation; but be of good cheer, I have overcome the world" (John 16:33).

2. **Accept that problems come in a variety of ways**

    Note that the Bible uses the word "many" to speak of the trials we will face in the following verse. It says in 1 Peter 1:6, "...You must endure many trials for a little while (New Living Translation)."

3. Accept that problems have a purpose

We are instructed as follows, "My brethren, count it all joy when you fall into various trials, knowing that the testing of your faith produces patience" (James 1:2–3). We must accept that problems can come as tests. Let us look at the story of Abraham again for the next example. Abraham was tested by God when he was asked to sacrifice his son Isaac. Abraham passed this great test because of his obedience to God's voice and his son's life was spared. But just imagine the grief he suffered knowing he was going to kill his son, the son of his great promise. God still tests people today. Next time you are presented with a difficult challenge, I encourage you to look at it as a test from God and consider how it can make you stronger.

4. Accept that problems come unexpectedly

Below is the beginning of a story in the Bible about a man who encountered difficult problems in his life.

[1]There was a man in the land of Uz, whose name *was* Job; and that man was blameless and upright, and one who feared God and shunned evil. [2]And seven sons and three daughters were born to him. [3]Also, his possessions were seven thousand sheep, three thousand camels, five hundred yoke of oxen, five hundred female donkeys, and a very large household, so that this man was the greatest of all the people of the East.

[4]And his sons would go and feast *in their* houses, each on his *appointed* day, and would send and invite their three sisters to eat and drink with them. [5]So it was, when the days of feasting had run their course, that Job would send and sanctify them, and he would rise early in the morning and

offer burnt offerings *according to* the number of them all. For Job said, "It may be that my sons have sinned and cursed God in their hearts." Thus Job did regularly.

Everything looked as if it were going right in Job's life. Job was upright and devoted to God. He had many possessions. He had a big family. Job was experiencing the best of the good life up until verse 5. Then everything started to change for Job.

Satan Attacks Job's Character

[6] Now there was a day when the sons of God came to present themselves before the LORD, and Satan also came among them. [7] And the LORD said to Satan, "From where do you come?"

So Satan answered the LORD and said, "From going to and fro on the earth, and from walking back and forth on it."

[8] Then the LORD said to Satan, "Have you considered My servant Job, that *there is* none like him on the earth, a blameless and upright man, one who fears God and shuns evil?"

[9] So Satan answered the LORD and said, "Does Job fear God for nothing? [10] Have You not made a hedge around him, around his household, and around all that he has on every side? You have blessed the work of his hands, and his possessions have increased in the land. [11] But now, stretch out Your hand and touch all that he has, and he will surely curse You to Your face!"

[12] And the LORD said to Satan, "Behold, all that he has *is* in your power; only do not lay a hand on his *person.*"

So Satan went out from the presence of the LORD.

Job loses his property and children

¹³ Now there was a day when his sons and daughters *were* eating and drinking wine in their oldest brother's house; ¹⁴ and a messenger came to Job and said, "The oxen were plowing and the donkeys feeding beside them, ¹⁵ when the Sabeans raided *them* and took them away—indeed they have killed the servants with the edge of the sword; and I alone have escaped to tell you!"

¹⁶ While he *was* still speaking, another also came and said, "The fire of God fell from heaven and burned up the sheep and the servants, and consumed them; and I alone have escaped to tell you!"

¹⁷ While he *was* still speaking, another also came and said, "The Chaldeans formed three bands, raided the camels and took them away, yes, and killed the servants with the edge of the sword; and I alone have escaped to tell you!"

¹⁸ While he *was* still speaking, another also came and said, "Your sons and daughters *were* eating and drinking wine in their oldest brother's house, ¹⁹ and suddenly a great wind came from across the wilderness and struck the four corners of the house, and it fell on the young people, and they are dead; and I alone have escaped to tell you!"

²⁰ Then Job arose, tore his robe, and shaved his head; and he fell to the ground and worshiped. ²¹ And he said:

"Naked I came from my mother's womb,
And naked shall I return there.
The LORD gave, and the LORD has taken away;

Blessed be the name of the LORD."

²² In all this Job did not sin nor charge God with wrong. (Job 1:1–22)

"¹Again there was a day when the sons of God came to present themselves before the LORD, and Satan came also among them to present himself before the LORD. ² And the LORD said to Satan, "From where do you come?"

Satan answered the LORD and said, "From going to and fro on the earth, and from walking back and forth on it."

³ Then the LORD said to Satan, "Have you considered My servant Job, that *there is* none like him on the earth, a blameless and upright man, one who fears God and shuns evil? And still he holds fast to his integrity, although you incited Me against him, to destroy him without cause."

⁴ So Satan answered the LORD and said, "Skin for skin! Yes, all that a man has he will give for his life. ⁵ But stretch out Your hand now, and touch his bone and his flesh, and he will surely curse You to Your face!"

⁶ And the LORD said to Satan, "Behold, he *is* in your hand, but spare his life."

⁷ So Satan went out from the presence of the LORD, and struck Job with painful boils from the sole of his foot to the crown of his head. ⁸ And he took for himself a potsherd with which to scrape himself while he sat in the midst of the ashes.

⁹ Then his wife said to him, "Do you still hold fast to your integrity? Curse God and die!"

¹⁰ But he said to her, "You speak as one of the foolish women speaks. Shall we indeed accept good from God, and shall we not accept adversity?" **In all this Job did not sin with his lips**. (Job 2:1–10)

If you look at the examples presented in this section, you can see that this man loved God even though he faced great trials. Job lost all of his property and children in almost an instant. Then he suffered a terrible skin disease that covered his whole body. But I love how Job reacted. The Bible says that in all of this he did not sin with his lips. Job knew that God was in control and he did not think himself too great to be afflicted. He never turned his back on God.

In the end, it turns out that because of Job's faithfulness to the Lord, God blessed him with double of what he had prior to his afflictions (Job 42:12–17). Our love for the Lord has a reward. A faithful man shall abound in blessings (Proverbs 28:20). Be prepared to face troubles in life so that when they happen you still trust in God.

Life Lessons:

- *There will be problems in life but these should not cause us to love God any less*

- *To love God above all is the greatest commandment we must keep*

Bible Study Discussion Questions:

1. Define love in your own words?

2. Who do you love the most and why?

3. What do you think are the reasons why God wants us to love Him with all our heart, with all our soul, and with all our mind?

4. Based on the lesson, how can we love God unconditionally?

5. What do you admire most in Job's character?

6. In the Bible, can you name a person or people who loved God and what happened in their lives? In contrast, a person or people who do not love God?

7. In the challenging times of our life, how can we keep on loving God despite problems or negative situations?

8. Based on the lesson and discussion, what can we apply in our daily life?

KEY 4

Obey God Above All

$\mathscr{I}$t is important to know why we must obey God above all and all of the time, without condition or limitation. Here I will discuss the main reasons.

Reasons why we must obey God

1. He is our Creator

The Bible says, "So God created man in His *own* image; in the image of God He created him; male and female He created them" (Genesis 1:27). You and I were created by God in His image. He knows us more than we know ourselves. God always desires the best for mankind because we are like an extension of Himself.

2. He loves us and only intends the best for us

God's word says, "For I know the thoughts that I think toward you, ...thoughts of peace and **not of evil**, to give you a future and a hope (Jeremiah 29:11). Just like it says in Part I of this book, God has great love for us. The ultimate extension of this was demonstrated by His sending His only Son to die for our sins (John 3:16). Because He loves us, we can be sure that God's commands for us were designed with good intentions.

3. He knows all things and His ways are perfect

Psalm 18:30 says, "As for God, His way is perfect; The word of the LORD is proven; He is a shield to all who trust in Him." God is perfect in all of His ways. Many people have tried to solve their problems by themselves, resulting in more problems. Multitudes have invested time, money and other resources into solving their problems but rather their problems grew worse. You are wise if you will seek God first and ask for His guidance. Whatever He commands comes from the best source possible, Himself.

My obedience to God's still small voice

One day at work after I worshipped and prayed, God the Holy Spirit spoke to my spirit to go to "apartment 1915." I said to the Lord, "They don't have a maintenance request." I tried to ignore it and focus on other things to do but then once again He spoke, telling me to go to "apartment 1915". The second time, I obeyed. I took my tool bag and went up to the apartment. (Amazing God! He even gives me the exact apartment number!)

I didn't know what was happening, so I first prayed in the stairwell of the building before knocking on the apartment door. As the resident opened the door, I said, "I would like to check the work I did last week to see if everything is okay." The resident willingly allowed me to enter and check the work done. As I entered the apartment, the Lord placed it on my heart to share story of the life of Job and other scriptures.

I shared the scriptures and the man appeared to be quite moved by it. He asked, "Why are you telling *me* this?" He went on, "I have not had anything to do with God since the death of my daughter 7 years ago." He had closed his heart concerning God. As I began to speak the words of Jesus, I could see it touched his heart and he in turn began to open up about his years of pain. He asked, "Why are you telling me all about this?" I shared about the pains of Job and how he responded by praising God despite the difficult situations. I believe the Lord used me to speak His words and they became a source of healing to the man. We ended the visit in prayer.

One week after that, I saw the very same man in the laundry room. He was whistling and was joyful. He had a joy that could be seen in the way he walked and he was even greeting other residents of the building. HE IS A CHANGED MAN.

I believe God used me to transform this man. I realized how much God loves this man. I did not know him but God knew him and loved him very much. If I had not obeyed the Holy Spirit, perhaps this man would not have come to realize this love God had for him. I rejoiced in having obeyed God's still small voice. Amazing God! He knows everything and loves every person.

The Obedience of the Prophet Samuel

When King Saul was rejected by God, God sent the prophet Samuel to Bethlehem to anoint one of Jesse's sons as his successor. This is what happened:

¹Now the LORD said to Samuel, "How long will you mourn for Saul, seeing I have rejected him from reigning over Israel? Fill your horn with oil, and go; I am sending you to Jesse the Bethlehemite. ***For I have provided Myself a king among his sons.*** " ² And Samuel said, "How can I go? If Saul hears *it,* he will kill me." But the LORD said, "Take a heifer with you, and say, 'I have come to sacrifice to the LORD.' ³ Then invite Jesse to the sacrifice, and I will show you what you shall do; you shall anoint for Me the one I name to you." ⁴ So Samuel did what the LORD said, and went to Bethlehem. And the elders of the town trembled at his coming, and said, "Do you come peaceably?" ⁵ And he said, "Peaceably; I have come to sacrifice to the LORD. Sanctify yourselves, and come with me to the sacrifice." Then he consecrated Jesse and his sons, and invited them to the sacrifice. ⁶ So it was, when they came, that he looked at Eliab and said, "Surely the LORD's anointed *is* before Him!" ⁷ But the LORD said to Samuel, ***"Do not look at his appearance or at his physical stature, because I have refused him. For the LORD does not see as man see^a for man looks at the outward appearance, but the LORD looks at the heart."*** ⁸ So Jesse called Abinadab, and made him pass before Samuel. And he said, "Neither has the LORD chosen this one." ⁹ Then Jesse made Shammah pass by. And he said, "Neither has the LORD chosen this one." ¹⁰ Thus Jesse made seven of his sons pass before Samuel. And Samuel said to Jesse, "The LORD has not chosen these." ¹¹ And Samuel said to Jesse, "Are all the young men here?" Then he said, ***"There remains yet the youngest, and there he is, keeping the sheep***." And Samuel said to Jesse, "Send and bring him. For we will not sit down till he comes here." ¹² So he sent and brought him in. Now he *was*

ruddy, with bright eyes, and good-looking. *And the LORD said, "Arise, anoint him; for this is the one!"* [13] Then Samuel took the horn of oil and anointed him in the midst of his brothers; and the Spirit of the LORD came upon David from that day forward. So Samuel arose and went to Ramah (1 Samuel 16:1–13)

At first, Samuel assumed that Eliab was the chosen person, but God judges the heart. Samuel obeyed God in choosing David even though he was the youngest son. Through Samuel's obedience, David became a great king and he wrote most of the book of Psalm. Under David's leadership, Israel defeated many nations and the Ark of the Covenant was brought to Jerusalem.

Obey Lord Jesus Always

*D*oes the Lord Jesus speak today? Yes! Nothing is impossible for our God. Even after He ascended to heaven, He spoke to Paul. This was while Paul was on his way to Damascus. Jesus chose and appointed people to serve in His kingdom. I personally know someone who was taught by the Lord. I have heard testimonies of people who have seen Jesus.

To live the abundant life, a person must obey Lord Jesus always. Let us read a story of a man who obeyed Jesus.

Ananias and Saul of Tarsus

The Lord Jesus had commanded His disciples to go and preach the Gospel when a man named Saul of Tarsus was persecuting the church. The bulk of His disciples feared Saul. But, what was the reaction of Ananias? Let us read Acts 9:10–19:

[10] Now there was a certain disciple at Damascus named Ananias; and to him the Lord said in a vision, "Ananias."

And he said, "Here I am, Lord."

[11] So the Lord *said* to him, "Arise and go to the street called Straight, and inquire at the house of Judas for *one* called Saul of Tarsus, for behold, he is praying. [12] And in a vision he has seen a man named Ananias coming in and putting *his* hand on him, so that he might receive his sight."

[13] Then Ananias answered, "Lord, I have heard from many about this man, how much harm he has done to Your saints in Jerusalem. [14] And here he has authority from the chief priests to bind all who call on Your name."

[15] But the Lord said to him, "Go, for he is a chosen vessel of Mine to bear My name before Gentiles, kings, and the children of Israel. [16] For I will show him how many things he must suffer for My name's sake."

[17] And Ananias went his way and entered the house; and laying his hands on him he said, "Brother Saul, the Lord Jesus, who appeared to you on the road as you came, has sent me that you may receive your sight and be filled with the Holy Spirit." [18] Immediately there fell from his eyes *something* like scales, and he received his sight at once; and he arose and was baptized.

[19] So when he had received food, he was strengthened. Then Saul spent some days with the disciples at Damascus. (Acts 9:10–19)

Ananias obeyed God even though he was fearful at the beginning. His obedience to Lord Jesus resulted in the infilling of the Holy Spirit of Saul who became known as the Apostle Paul. Apostle Paul became one of the most influential individuals in church history. He was used mightily by the Lord. He became a successful missionary. He wrote the foundational documents for the Christian faith. The New Testament letters he wrote changed the lives of millions, even billions, of people.

Simon and the Great Catch of Fish

Let's read another story about a man's obedience that brought blessings to himself and others.

> [1]One day as Jesus was standing by the Lake of Gennesaret, the people were crowding around him and listening to the word of God. [2]He saw at the water's edge two boats, left there by the fishermen, who were washing their nets. [3]He got into one of the boats, the one belonging to Simon, and asked him to put out a little from shore. Then he sat down and taught the people from the boat.
>
> [4]When he had finished speaking, he said to Simon, "Put out into deep water, and let down the nets for a catch."
>
> [5]Simon answered, "Master, we've worked hard all night and haven't caught anything. But because you say so, I will let down the nets."
>
> [6]When they had done so, they caught such a large number of fish that their nets began to break. [7]So they signaled their partners in the other boat to come and help them, and they came and filled both boats so full that they began to sink.
>
> [8]When Simon Peter saw this, he fell at Jesus' knees and said, "Go away from me, Lord; I am a sinful man!" [9]For he and all his companions were astonished at the catch of fish they had taken, [10]and so were James and John, the sons of Zebedee, Simon's partners.
>
> Then Jesus said to Simon, "Don't be afraid; from now on you will fish for people." [11]So they pulled their boats up on shore, left everything and followed him. (Luke 5: 1–11)

Peter was an experienced fisherman but chose to obey Jesus. In man's eyes, Peter was more skilled. But we can see here that Peter reacted differently than most men would have. Peter did not say, "I am more familiar with fishing. I don't need your advice, thank you." **But Peter chose to obey Jesus** by saying, "…But because you say so, I will let down the nets."

Peter had an obedient heart. He overcame his doubts and he chose to obey. What was the result of Peter's obedience? Well, they caught a great catch of fish. But even more, Peter got a firsthand glimpse of the Lord's power.

Jesus turned an empty boat to a full one. We, like Peter, must recognize that obeying God is the wisest course of action. Perhaps you hesitate to obey because you fear the consequences.

Remember that the same sovereign, all-powerful and all-knowing God who keeps your heart beating and the planets orbiting is more than able to handle any negative results of your obedience.

Obedience that extends to others

In obeying God to open up a Bible study in our home, God has enabled us to bless others. We met a man who suffered from depression and was hospitalized because of his separation from his wife and children.

From the first time we met him, we knew something was wrong in his life. He attended our Bible Study meetings and came to accept Jesus as his Lord and Savior. He was later baptized.

In one of our Bible study meetings, he made a prayer request. He wanted to see his children again but the authorities would not allow him to be near them.

We prayed together, believing God to intervene in the situation. Later, we learned he received a notice to see his youngest son for a few minutes. He went and saw his son.

As he faithfully sought God, the Lord opened the way for him to eventually see his whole family. I was there with him when he saw his family after months of separation.

Lord Jesus opened the way for this man to be with his children.

The results of obedience will surprise you and you will be a blessing to others. When we obey Lord Jesus we will never be disappointed.

Obey God the Holy Spirit Always

$\mathcal{L}$ord Jesus delivered this important message to His disciples, "… The Helper, the Holy Spirit, whom the Father will send in My name, He will teach you all things, and bring to your remembrance all things that I said to you" (John 14:26).

Who is The Holy Spirit? Acts 1:8 says, "But you shall receive power when the Holy Spirit has come upon you; and you shall be witnesses to Me in Jerusalem, and in all Judea and Samaria, and to the end of the earth." He always refers to the Holy Spirit with the masculine pronoun "He." The Holy Spirit is a Person who lives in the believer. John 14:17 describes Him saying, "…The Spirit of truth, whom the world cannot receive, because it neither sees Him nor knows Him; but you know Him, for He dwells with you and will be in you."

The Holy Spirit came into the world to have the same fellowship as Lord Jesus with His disciples.

Facts about the Holy Spirit

1. He is a holy Person who comes to dwell in our lives

2. He knows our thoughts

3. He hears every word we say

4. He sees our behavior

5. He is a divine Person who is willing to use us according to His perfect will

6. He in the omnipotent, omnipresent and omniscient God

God the Holy Spirit guides the believer

God the Holy Spirit communicates to the believer to accomplish His will. Here is a story that shows how the Holy Spirit worked to bring the gospel to an Ethiopian eunuch.

[26] Now an angel of the Lord spoke to Philip, saying, "Arise and go toward the south along the road which goes down from Jerusalem to Gaza." This is desert. [27] So he arose and went. And behold, a man of Ethiopia, a eunuch of great authority under Candace the queen of the Ethiopians, who had charge of all her treasury, and had come to Jerusalem to worship, [28] was returning. And sitting in his chariot, he was reading Isaiah the prophet. [29] **Then the Spirit said to Philip, "Go near and overtake this chariot."** [30] So Philip ran to him, and heard him reading the prophet Isaiah, and said, "Do you understand what you are reading?" [31] And he said, "How can I, unless someone guides me?" And he asked Philip to come up and sit with him. [32] The place in the Scripture which he read was this:

"He was led as a sheep to the slaughter; And as a lamb before its shearer is silent, So He opened not His mouth. [33] *In His humiliation His justice was taken away, And who will declare His generation? For His life is taken from the earth."*

[34] So the eunuch answered Philip and said, "I ask you, of whom does the prophet say this, of himself or of some other man?" [35] Then Philip opened his mouth, and beginning at this Scripture, preached Jesus to him. [36] Now as they went down the road, they came to some water. And the eunuch said, "See, *here is* water. What hinders me from being baptized?" [37] Then Philip said, "If you believe with all your heart, you may." And he answered and said, "I believe that Jesus Christ is the Son of God."[38] So he commanded the

chariot to stand still. And both Philip and the eunuch went down into the water, and he baptized him. [39] Now when they came up out of the water, the Spirit of the Lord caught Philip away, so that the eunuch saw him no more; and he went on his way rejoicing. [40] But Philip was found at Azotus. And passing through, he preached in all the cities till he came to Caesarea. (Acts 8:26–40)

In this account, the Holy Spirit directed Philip to overtake the chariot. Philip opened the conversation with a question, "Do you understand what you are reading?"

Because of Philip's obedience to the Spirit, a eunuch of great authority came to understand the Scripture. The eunuch was saved and baptized with water and went on his way rejoicing.

Consequences of Disobedience

Genesis chapter 3 shares an important story of how mankind was deceived and fell into sin by disobeying God. Let us read Genesis 3:1–13:

[1] Now the serpent was more cunning than any beast of the field which the Lord God had made. And he said to the woman, "Has God indeed said, 'You shall not eat of every tree of the garden'?"

[2] And the woman said to the serpent, "We may eat the fruit of the trees of the garden; [3] but of the fruit of the tree which is in the midst of the garden, God has said, 'You shall not eat it, nor shall you touch it, lest you die.'"

[4] Then the serpent said to the woman, "You will not surely die. [5] For God knows that in the day you eat of it your eyes will be opened, and you will be like God, knowing good and evil."

[6] So when the woman saw that the tree was good for food, that it was pleasant to the eyes, and a tree desirable to make one wise, she took of its fruit and ate. She also gave to her husband with her, and he ate. [7] Then the eyes of

both of them were opened, and they knew that they were naked; and they sewed fig leaves together and made themselves coverings.

[8] And they heard the sound of the Lord God walking in the garden in the cool of the day, and Adam and his wife hid themselves from the presence of the Lord God among the trees of the garden.

[9] Then the Lord God called to Adam and said to him, "Where are you?"

[10] So he said, "I heard Your voice in the garden, and I was afraid because I was naked; and I hid myself."

[11] And He said, "Who told you that you were naked? Have you eaten from the tree of which I commanded you that you should not eat?"

[12] Then the man said, "The woman whom You gave to be with me, she gave me of the tree, and I ate."

[13] And the Lord God said to the woman, "What is this you have done?"

The woman said, "The serpent deceived me, and I ate." (Genesis 3:1–13)

What are the consequences of disobedience? Let us consider the following aspects of the passage:

1. Fear comes: In verse 8, the first instance of fear is described as Adam and Eve hid themselves from God.

2. We find ourselves blaming others for sin: In verses 12 and 13, both Adam and Eve blame others for their sin.

3. The land is cursed: Verse 17 which follows the selected passage says, "Cursed *is* the ground for your sake..."

4. Murder happens: Genesis chapter 4 tells how Adam and Eve's first son, Cain, murdered their second son, Abel. This would not have happened if Adam and Eve did not disobey God.

5. Wickedness increases: Genesis 6 describes widespread wickedness among mankind.

6. The Lord regrets creating mankind: The Lord was sorry that He had made man by Genesis 6 (Genesis 6:6).

7. Death ensues: Adam and Eve died. This is what God said would happen as a result of their disobedience (Genesis 3:19) and God's word is always true.

Matthew 24 lists other consequences of sin:

- Wars
- Earthquakes
- Famine
- Pestilence
- Lawlessness
- Unfriendliness ("The love of many will grow cold")
- Hate
- Betrayal

Important!

If Adam and Eve could have seen the future of their decision to disobey God, I believe they would NOT have disobeyed God. For us this is very important. We must set our hearts on obeying God no matter what the opposition may be. Even if it will cost our lives to obey God, we must choose to obey God. God can enable us if we are willing to obey Him. We will be rewarded for our obedience.

Life Lessons:

- *God will always tell us the right thing to do even when we don't understand it in the moment*

- *We do not have to worry about any negative consequences of obedience because God will take care of these*

- *Our obedience to Lord Jesus can lead to great things we cannot even imagine*

- *There is joy to be experienced in our obedience to God*

Bible Study Discussion Questions:

1. Based on the lesson, what are the reasons we must obey God unconditionally?

2. As discussed, what are the results of Prophet Samuel's obedience?

3. As discussed, what are the results of Ananias' obedience?

4. As discussed, what are the results of Peter's obedience?

5. Who is the Holy Spirit? Why is He important in our life? Why is it important to obey Him?

6. In the Bible, can you name a person who obeyed God? What was the result of his/her obedience?

7. Disobedience has painful consequences. In the Bible, do you know a person who disobeyed God and what happened to him/her?

8. In this ungodly world we live in, how can we keep on obeying God in spite of difficult situations?

9. Based on the lesson and discussion, what can we apply in our daily life?

KEY 5

Fear God Above All

*W*ho do you fear the most? Is it your father, your mother, your boss, the police or armed robbers? To live the abundant life God has for us we must fear Him above any person or created being.

King Solomon's final words in the book of Ecclesiastes were as follows:

> [13] Let us hear the conclusion of the whole matter: Fear God and keep His commandments, for this is man's all. [14] For God will bring every work into judgment, including every secret thing, whether good or evil. (Ecclesiastes 12:13–14)

We must fear God because He is judge over all. He sees everything. The word of God says:

> "Am I a God who is near," declares the LORD, "And not a God far off? "Can a man hide himself in hiding places So I do not see him?" declares the LORD. "Do I not fill the heavens and the earth?" declares the LORD. (Jeremiah 23:23–24 NASB)

The Bible also says that the eyes of the LORD are in every place, watching the evil and the good (Proverbs 15:3).

The great mistake of King Saul

Here is a story about a great mistake made by King Saul that illustrates how our life goes off course when we fail to fear God above others:

> [1] Samuel also said to Saul, "The LORD sent me to anoint you king over His people, over Israel. Now therefore, heed the voice of the words of the LORD. [2] Thus says the LORD of hosts: 'I will punish Amalek *for* what he did to Israel, how he ambushed him on the way when he came up from Egypt. [3] Now go and attack Amalek, and utterly destroy all that they have, and do not spare them. But kill both man and woman,

infant and nursing child, ox and sheep, camel and donkey.'"

⁴ So Saul gathered the people together and numbered them in Telaim, two hundred thousand foot soldiers and ten thousand men of Judah. ⁵ And Saul came to a city of Amalek, and lay in wait in the valley.

⁶ Then Saul said to the Kenites, "Go, depart, get down from among the Amalekites, lest I destroy you with them. For you showed kindness to all the children of Israel when they came up out of Egypt." So the Kenites departed from among the Amalekites. ⁷ And Saul attacked the Amalekites, from Havilah all the way to Shur, which is east of Egypt. ⁸ He also took Agag king of the Amalekites alive, and utterly destroyed all the people with the edge of the sword. ⁹ But Saul and the people spared Agag and the best of the sheep, the oxen, the fatlings, the lambs, and all *that was* good, and were unwilling to utterly destroy them. But everything despised and worthless, that they utterly destroyed.

¹⁰ Now the word of the LORD came to Samuel, saying, ¹¹ "I greatly regret that I have set up Saul *as* king, for he has turned back from following Me, and has not performed My commandments." And it grieved Samuel, and he cried out to the LORD all night. ¹² So when Samuel rose early in the morning to meet Saul, it was told Samuel, saying, "Saul went to Carmel, and indeed, he set up a monument for himself; and he has gone on around, passed by, and gone down to Gilgal." ¹³ Then Samuel went to Saul, and Saul said to him, "Blessed *are* you of the LORD! I have performed the commandment of the LORD."

[14] But Samuel said, "What then *is* this bleating of the sheep in my ears, and the lowing of the oxen which I hear?"

[15] And Saul said, "They have brought them from the Amalekites; for the people spared the best of the sheep and the oxen, to sacrifice to the LORD your God; and the rest we have utterly destroyed."

[16] Then Samuel said to Saul, "Be quiet! And I will tell you what the LORD said to me last night."

And he said to him, "Speak on."

[17] So Samuel said, "When you *were* little in your own eyes, *were* you not head of the tribes of Israel? And did not the LORD anoint you king over Israel? [18] Now the LORD sent you on a mission, and said, 'Go, and utterly destroy the sinners, the Amalekites, and fight against them until they are consumed.' [19] Why then did you not obey the voice of the LORD? Why did you swoop down on the spoil, and do evil in the sight of the LORD?"

[20] And Saul said to Samuel, "But I have obeyed the voice of the LORD, and gone on the mission on which the LORD sent me, and brought back Agag king of Amalek; I have utterly destroyed the Amalekites. [21] But the people took of the plunder, sheep and oxen, the best of the things which should have been utterly destroyed, to sacrifice to the LORD your God in Gilgal."

[22] So Samuel said:

"Has the LORD *as great* delight in burnt offerings and sacrifices, As in obeying the voice of the LORD?
Behold, to obey is better than sacrifice, *And* to heed than the fat of rams.
[23] For rebellion *is as* the sin of witchcraft, And stubbornness *is as* iniquity and idolatry.

Because you have rejected the word of the LORD, He also has rejected you from *being* king."

²⁴ Then Saul said to Samuel, **"I have sinned**, for I have transgressed the commandment of the LORD and your words, **because I feared the people and obeyed their voice**. ²⁵ Now therefore, please pardon my sin, and return with me, that I may worship the LORD."

²⁶ But Samuel said to Saul, "I will not return with you, for you have rejected the word of the LORD, and the LORD has rejected you from being king over Israel."

²⁷ And as Samuel turned around to go away, *Saul* seized the edge of his robe, and it tore. ²⁸ So Samuel said to him, "The LORD has torn the kingdom of Israel from you today, and has given it to a neighbor of yours, *who is* better than you. ²⁹ And also the Strength of Israel will not lie nor relent. For He *is* not a man, that He should relent."

³⁰ Then he said, "I have sinned; *yet* honor me now, please, before the elders of my people and before Israel, and return with me, that I may worship the LORD your God." ³¹ So Samuel turned back after Saul, and Saul worshiped the LORD.

³² Then Samuel said, "Bring Agag king of the Amalekites here to me." So Agag came to him cautiously.

And Agag said, "Surely the bitterness of death is past."

³³ But Samuel said, "As your sword has made women childless, so shall your mother be childless among women." And Samuel hacked Agag in pieces before the LORD in Gilgal.

³⁴ Then Samuel went to Ramah, and Saul went up to his house at Gibeah of Saul. ³⁵ And Samuel went no more to see Saul until the day of his death. Nevertheless Samuel mourned for Saul, and the LORD regretted that He had made Saul king over Israel. (1 Samuel 15)

Saul did not fear God enough to do exactly as God had instructed him. True Godly fear would have caused Saul to destroy *everything,* including all the animals, just as God had commanded him. Instead, Saul let some of the animals of the Amalekites live.

The results of fearing people

Fearing people over God has particular kinds of consequences. Below are some of those that were experienced by Saul as a result of his failure to fear God more than others:

1. Rejection from God's service (verse 26)

2. Removal from authority (verse 28)

3. Shifting of God's anointing to another servant (verse 28)

4. Withdrawal of Godly council (verse 35)

5. God's regret (verse 35)

In our life we will hear many voices that can hinder us from making the decision to fear God. **We must be wise to follow God and not people**. God's word is here to guide us. God the Holy Spirit is living in every born-again believer to help us to make the right decisions in life. We must not be afraid of people, for the Bible says, "And do not fear those who kill the body but cannot kill the soul. But rather fear Him who is able to destroy both soul and body in hell" (Matthew 10:28).

Abraham's fear of God

Abraham feared God. Let us read Genesis 22:1–19:

¹ Now it came to pass after these things that God tested Abraham, and said to him, "Abraham!"

And he said, "Here I am."

² Then He said, "Take now your son, your only *son* Isaac, whom you love, and go to the land of Moriah, and offer

him there as a burnt offering on one of the mountains of which I shall tell you."

³ So Abraham rose early in the morning and saddled his donkey, and took two of his young men with him, and Isaac his son; and he split the wood for the burnt offering, and arose and went to the place of which God had told him. ⁴ Then on the third day Abraham lifted his eyes and saw the place afar off. ⁵ And Abraham said to his young men, "Stay here with the donkey; the lad and I will go yonder and worship, and we will come back to you."

⁶ So Abraham took the wood of the burnt offering and laid *it* on Isaac his son; and he took the fire in his hand, and a knife, and the two of them went together. ⁷ But Isaac spoke to Abraham his father and said, "My father!"

And he said, "Here I am, my son."

Then he said, "Look, the fire and the wood, but where *is* the lamb for a burnt offering?"

⁸ And Abraham said, "My son, God will provide for Himself the lamb for a burnt offering." So the two of them went together.

⁹ Then they came to the place of which God had told him. And Abraham built an altar there and placed the wood in order; and he bound Isaac his son and laid him on the altar, upon the wood. ¹⁰ And Abraham stretched out his hand and took the knife to slay his son.

¹¹ But the Angel of the LORD called to him from heaven and said, "Abraham, Abraham!"

So he said, "Here I am."

¹² And He said, "Do not lay your hand on the lad, or do anything to him; for now I know that you fear God, since you have not withheld your son, your only *son,* from Me."

¹³ Then Abraham lifted his eyes and looked, and there behind *him was* a ram caught in a thicket by its horns. So Abraham went and took the ram, and offered it up for a

burnt offering instead of his son. [14] And Abraham called the name of the place, The-LORD-Will-Provide; as it is said *to* this day, "In the Mount of the LORD it shall be provided."

[15] Then the Angel of the LORD called to Abraham a second time out of heaven, [16] and said: "By Myself I have sworn, says the LORD, because you have done this thing, and have not withheld your son, your only *son*— [17] blessing I will bless you, and multiplying I will multiply your descendants as the stars of the heaven and as the sand which *is* on the seashore; and your descendants shall possess the gate of their enemies. [18] In your seed all the nations of the earth shall be blessed, because you have obeyed My voice." [19] So Abraham returned to his young men, and they rose and went together to Beersheba; and Abraham dwelt at Beersheba.

How did God know that Abraham feared Him? In verse 12 it said, "…for now I know that you fear God, since you have not withheld your son, your only *son,* from Me." God rewarded Abraham with great promises in verses 16, 17 and 18.

The benefits of fearing God

Here are some of the benefits of fearing God with supporting Scriptures that are good to remember.

1. **The secret of the Lord is revealed**

   "The secret of the Lord is with those who fear Him, And He will show them His covenant." (Psalm 25:14)

2. **There is heavenly protection**

   "The angel of the Lord encamps all around those who fear Him, And delivers them." (Psalm 34:7)

3. **Wisdom is granted**

   "The fear of the Lord is the beginning of wisdom; A good understanding have all those who do His commandments. His praise endures forever." (Psalm 111:10)

"The fear of the Lord is the beginning of knowledge, But fools despise wisdom and instruction." (Proverbs 1:7)

4. Blessings are released

"Blessed is everyone who fears the Lord, Who walks in His ways." (Psalm 128:1)

5. There is a lengthening of days (long life)

"The fear of the Lord prolongs days, But the years of the wicked will be shortened." (Proverbs 10:27)

6. There is strong confidence

"In the fear of the Lord there is strong confidence, And His children will have a place of refuge." (Proverbs 14:26)

"The fear of man brings a snare, But whoever trusts in the Lord shall be safe." (Proverbs 29:25)

7. There are riches, honor and life

"By humility and the fear of the Lord are riches and honor and life." (Proverbs 22:4)

8. The gift of salvation is made available

Cornelius was "A devout man and one who feared God with all his household (Acts 10:2)." In the story of the Apostle Peter and Cornelius in Acts 10:1–48, the fear of God led to his salvation.

The Bible also says, "Wisdom and knowledge will be the stability of your times, And the strength of salvation; The fear of the Lord is His treasure." (Isaiah 33:6)

It is a command that all men must fear the Lord. The Bible says, "Let all the earth fear the Lord; Let all the inhabitants of the world stand in awe of Him" (Psalm 33:8).

Life Lessons:

- *We must remember that our ways are not hidden from God*

- *God will judge us according to our works*

- *There are many blessings that come with fearing God*

Bible Study Discussion Questions:

1. Based on the topic, what was the great mistake of King Saul?

2. What are the consequences of King Saul's disobedience?

3. How did God know that Abraham feared Him?

4. What are the benefits of fearing God?

5. In this sinful generation, why do you think people have lost the fear of God?

6. In the Bible, can you name a person who showed his/her fear of God and tell what happened as a result? In contrast, can you name a person or people who have no fear of God and what happened as a result?

7. In our present society, how can we keep on fearing God despite opposition or challenging situations?

8. Based on the lesson and discussion, what can we apply to our daily life?

KEY 6

Keep God's Commandments

John 14:21

"He who has My commandments and keeps them, it is he who loves Me. And he who loves Me will be loved by My Father, and I will love him and manifest Myself to him."

$\mathcal{J}$esus said, "If you love Me, Keep my commandments" (John 14:15). Not only does our keeping His commandments satisfy Him because it is proof of our love for Him, but we stand to gain from it. He provides benefits for us as we keep His commandments. The word "if" is conditional. This means that we will prove our love to Jesus only if we keep His commandments. Let us consider the blessings we can receive by keeping God's commandments. This is a passage from Deuteronomy:

[1] "Now it shall come to pass, if you diligently obey the voice of the Lord your God, to observe carefully all His commandments which I command you today, that the Lord your God will set you high above all nations of the earth. [2] And all these blessings shall come upon you and overtake you, because you obey the voice of the Lord your God:

[3] "Blessed *shall* you *be* in the city, and blessed *shall* you *be* in the country.

[4] "Blessed *shall be* the fruit of your body, the produce of your ground and the increase of your herds, the increase of your cattle and the offspring of your flocks.

[5] "Blessed *shall be* your basket and your kneading bowl.

[6] "Blessed *shall* you *be* when you come in, and blessed *shall* you *be* when you go out.

[7] "The Lord will cause your enemies who rise against you to be defeated before your face; they shall come out against you one way and flee before you seven ways.

[8] "The Lord will command the blessing on you in your storehouses and in all to which you set your hand, and He will bless you in the land which the Lord your God is giving you.

[9] "The Lord will establish you as a holy people to Himself, just as He has sworn to you, if you keep the commandments of the Lord your God and walk in His ways. [10] Then all peoples of the earth shall see that you are

called by the name of the Lord, and they shall be afraid of you. [11] And the Lord will grant you plenty of goods, in the fruit of your body, in the increase of your livestock, and in the produce of your ground, in the land of which the Lord swore to your fathers to give you. [12] The Lord will open to you His good treasure, the heavens, to give the rain to your land in its season, and to bless all the work of your hand. You shall lend to many nations, but you shall not borrow. [13] And the Lord will make you the head and not the tail; you shall be above only, and not be beneath, if you heed the commandments of the Lord your God, which I command you today, and are careful to observe *them.* [14] So you shall not turn aside from any of the words which I command you this day, *to* the right or the left, to go after other gods to serve them." (Deuteronomy 28:1–14)

Our good God does not stop there. As we will see, His blessings are many for those who keep His commandments.

Let us consider one of the great heroes of the Bible, King David. He was known as 'a man after God's own heart' (Acts 13:22). One of the main reasons he pleased God is because he kept God's commandments.

Psalms of David

Let us see some of the Psalms of King David.

- Psalm 18:21–22 says, "For I have kept the ways of the Lord, And have not wickedly departed from my God. For all His judgments were before me, And I did not put away His statutes from me."

- Psalm 12:6 says, "The words of the Lord are pure words, Like silver tried in a furnace of earth, Purified seven times."

- Psalm 19:9 says, "The judgments of the Lord are true and righteous altogether."

- Psalm 19:8 tells us that, "The statutes of the Lord are right, rejoicing the heart; The commandment of the Lord is pure, enlightening the eyes…"

- Psalm 37:34 says to, "Wait on the Lord, And keep His way, And He shall exalt you to inherit the land; When the wicked are cut off, you shall see it."

King David treasured the commandments of God. One scripture I love to meditate on is found in Psalm 119:11. It says, "Your word I have hidden in my heart, That I might not sin against You." The Psalmist hid the word of God in his heart for him not to sin against God. It should be our goal in life to read, meditate and hide the word of God in our hearts.

God's blessing to David

Psalm 89:34–35 says, "My covenant I will not break, Nor alter the word that has gone out of My lips. Once I have sworn by My holiness; I will not lie to David." The Lord established a covenant with David.

Here we will consider how God dealt with David's descendants. After David's death, his son Solomon reigned as king:

> "Because they have forsaken Me, and worshiped Ashtoreth the goddess of the Sidonians, Chemosh the god of the Moabites, and Milcom the god of the people of Ammon, and have not walked in My ways to do what is right in My eyes and keep My statutes and My judgments, as did his father David. However I will not take the whole kingdom out of his hand, because I have made him ruler all the days of his life **for the sake of My servant David**, whom I chose because he kept My commandments and My statutes." (1 Kings 11:33–34)

One hundred thirty years after David's death Jehoram reigns in Judah.

> "[16]Now in the fifth year of Joram the son of Ahab, king of Israel, Jehoshaphat having been king of Judah, Jehoram the son of Jehoshaphat began to reign as king of Judah. [17] He was thirty-two years old when he became king, and he reigned eight years in Jerusalem. [18] And he walked in the way of the kings of Israel, just as the house of Ahab had done, for the daughter of Ahab was his wife; and he did evil in the sight of the Lord. [19] Yet the Lord would

not destroy Judah, **for the sake of His servant David**, as He promised him to give a lamp to him and his sons forever." (2 Kings 8:16–19)

Two hundred sixty years after God's covenant with David still stands.

"⁵Return and tell Hezekiah the leader of My people, 'Thus says the Lord, the God of David your father: "I have heard your prayer, I have seen your tears; surely I will heal you. On the third day you shall go up to the house of the Lord. ⁶ And I will add to your days fifteen years. I will deliver you and this city from the hand of the king of Assyria; and I will defend this city for My own sake, and **for the sake of My servant David**.""" (2 Kings 20:5–6)

God's blessing to David extended to all his descendants. **We can give our children the best gift in life, which is God's favor, by keeping the commandments of God.**

We must keep the ways of the Lord even in difficult times in order to receive His wonderful generational blessings. Always remember that Almighty God is the true source of the wonderful blessings of life. No man can give as God gives. No man can provide as God provides. No man can keep a promise as God keeps a promise because God cannot lie.

Benefits from keeping God's commandments

Here are some more blessings we can receive from keeping God's commandments.

1. **Great peace**

   The Bible tells us, "Great peace have those who love Your law, And nothing causes them to stumble" (Psalm 119:165).

2. **Long life**

   In the book of Deuteronomy, the Bible tells us that keeping God's commandments can lead to a long life. "You shall therefore keep His statutes and His commandments which I command you today, that it may go well with you and with your children after you, and that you may prolong your days in the land which the Lord your God is giving you for all time" (Deuteronomy 4:40).

In Deuteronomy, Moses says to the Israelites that the Lord commanded that His commandments be taught, "That you may fear the Lord your God, to keep all His statutes and His commandments which I command you, you and your son and your grandson, all the days of your life, and that your days may be prolonged" (Deuteronomy 6:2).

3. **Abiding in God's love**

You are promised by Jesus in the book of John, that, "If you keep My commandments, you will abide in My love, just as I have kept My Father's commandments and abide in His love" (John 15:10).

4. **Ability to love others**

The Bible also says, "By this we know that we love the children of God, when we love God and keep His commandments" (1 John 5:2).

5. **Abiding in Jesus**

We abide in Jesus as He abides in us who keep His commandments. This is made clear in 1 John 3:24, which says, "Now he who keeps His commandments abides in Him, and He in him. And by this we know that He abides in us, by the Spirit whom He has given us."

6. **Answered prayer**

1 John 3:22 says, "And whatever we ask we receive from Him, because we keep His

commandments and do those things that are pleasing in His sight."

7. **Relationship with God**

The Bible says, "Now by this we know that we know Him, if we keep His commandments" (1 John 2:3).

Life Lessons:

- *There is a blessing of abundance which comes when you keep God's commandments*

- *Keeping God's commandments can bring blessings in your life and in the lives of your descendants even many generations after you are gone*

Bible Study Discussion Questions:

1. As explained, what are the blessings of keeping God's commandment?

2. Cite a verse in keeping God's commandment that you like and tell why?

3. As mentioned, how did God deal with David's descendants?

4. Why do you think many people in this generation have forgotten or doubt the commandments of God?

5. In the Bible, do you remember a person who kept God's commandments and what was his/her reward? In contrast, do you remember a person or people who did not keep God's commandments and what happened?

6. In this sinful generation, how can we keep on keeping God's commandments despite challenging situations?

7. Based on the lesson and discussion, what can we apply in our daily life?

KEY 7

Focus on God and Trust in Him

Isaiah 26:3

"You will keep *him* in perfect peace, *Whose* mind *is* stayed *on You,* Because he trusts in You."

$\mathscr{G}$od has made perfect peace in this troubled world available if we will focus on Him and trust in Him. Always remember He alone is God and there is no other. "Be still and know that I am God..." (Psalm 46:10). If you will diligently search the Scriptures, they will point you to only one Creator God. He is all powerful. He knows the end from the beginning. Nothing is impossible for Him that's why we can have perfect peace. He controls the events in history. He does not change. He cannot fail. He declares the end story of Satan and his demons—because He alone is God.

Focus on God

$\mathscr{I}$ remember the day when I was completely focused on myself and the things I want to accomplish in life. My mind had no peace. I would think about this and that... I worried about just about everything. It was a hard life to live. I ended up in a hospital room worrying about things and people in my life. I learned my lesson. Doing it my way is not the best way.

Focusing on God and His word means that our mind is stayed on God. Our mind is meditating the word of God day and night.

Below are scriptures about focusing on God.

Set your mind on things above, not on things on the earth. (Colossians 3:2)

"**But my eyes are fixed on you**, Sovereign Lord; in you I take refuge—do not give me over to death." (Psalm 141:8 NIV)

"...We do this by **keeping our eyes on Jesus**, the champion who initiates and perfects our faith. Because of the joy awaiting him, he endured the cross, disregarding its shame. Now he is seated in the place of honor beside God's throne." (Hebrews 12:2 NLT)

Can I focus on God and His word and be successful? My answer is definitely yes! It is actually the best way for us to live. One of my favorite scriptures says, "This Book of the Law shall not depart from your mouth, but you shall meditate in it day and night, that you may observe to do according to all that is written in it. For then you will make your way prosperous, and then you will have good success" (Joshua 1:8). The pathway for our success and prosperity is by meditating on God's word (the Bible) day and night then by being doers of the Word not hearers only.

Let us consider this wonderful story:

Jesus Walks on the Sea

> [22] Immediately Jesus made His disciples get into the boat and go before Him to the other side, while He sent the multitudes away. [23] And when He had sent the multitudes away, He went up on the mountain by Himself to pray. Now when evening came, He was alone there. [24] But the boat was now in the middle of the sea, tossed by the waves, for the wind was contrary.
>
> [25] Now in the fourth watch of the night Jesus went to them, walking on the sea. [26] And when the disciples saw Him walking on the sea, they were troubled, saying, "It is a ghost!" And they cried out for fear.
>
> [27] But immediately Jesus spoke to them, saying, "Be of good cheer! It is I; do not be afraid."
>
> [28] And Peter answered Him and said, "Lord, if it is You, command me to come to You on the water."
>
> [29] So He said, "Come." And when Peter had come down out of the boat, he walked on the water to go to Jesus. [30] But when he saw that the wind *was* boisterous, he was afraid; and beginning to sink he cried out, saying, "Lord, save me!"

³¹ And immediately Jesus stretched out *His* hand and caught him, and said to him, "O you of little faith, why did you doubt?" ³² And when they got into the boat, the wind ceased.

³³ Then those who were in the boat came and worshiped Him, saying, "Truly You are the Son of God." (Matthew 14:22–33)

What enabled Peter to walk on the water? First, was the command of the Lord Jesus to "Come," then Peter's focus on Jesus. Did Peter walk on the water? Yes! If Peter continued focusing on Jesus he would have reached Him. With God, all things are possible. If we keep our eyes on God and His word we can accomplish great things. God is the source of all life. He is the sustainer of universe.

Is God speaking to you to do things that are impossible? I encourage you to obey and keep your focus on Him. He will help you step by step. He will reward your obedience. Focusing or staying our mind on God is a lifetime journey. We may be distracted from time to time but God is faithful to complete what He started in us. His faithfulness endures forever. *He is the only one who does not lie and who does not fail.* His love never ends. Try God. You will be amazed at how good and wonderful He is. He is a loving and perfect Father.

One word from the Lord can give you a breakthrough in life. He loves you and wants you to be successful. Remember that His ways are perfect. We cannot improve on His ways because *He always acts in love and by His absolute perfect knowledge about everything.* Everything that concerns you and I He knows. Nothing is difficult for our God.

What distracted the focus of Peter in the story? The boisterous wind frightened him, and then Peter started to become afraid and then began to sink. **The boisterous wind can represent anything**

or anyone that distracts our focus on God. The Devil wants you to focus on your problems and difficulties in life. The enemy wants you defeated, so his army will work to distract you. You and I will encounter challenges while we are on Earth. Our life is not free from the enemy. We have to stand strong in faith towards God and His word.

Daily reading of the word of God is a must. It will give us our daily strength to endure the race God has set for us. I bought the whole Bible on MP3 and CD so that I could continue to listen and meditate. There are many good authors and preachers that can help you to focus on God. Ask God for good Christian mentors to help you.

I pray that you will keep your eye on Jesus. I believe you will be successful. You are able to overcome any challenges through Christ.

Trust in God

*F*ocusing on God and Trusting in God must go together so that we can maintain perfect peace.

Who do you trust the most? Trust means a firm belief or assured reliance in the reliability, truth, ability or strength of someone or something. Do you trust in others when you should be trusting in God?

Below is a short passage from the book of Psalm that gives reasons why we must put our trust in God:

> [7] The law of the Lord *is* perfect, converting the soul; The testimony of the Lord *is* sure, making wise the simple; [8] The statutes of the Lord *are* right, rejoicing the heart; The commandment of the Lord *is* pure, enlightening the eyes; [9] The fear of the Lord *is* clean, enduring forever; The judgments of the Lord *are* true *and* righteous altogether. [10] More to be desired *are they* than gold, Yea, than much fine gold; Sweeter also than honey and the honeycomb. [11] Moreover by them Your servant is warned, *And* in keeping them *there is* great reward. (Psalm 19:7–11)

We do our best to abide with human laws, how much more should we abide in the law of God which is perfect and proven! Every person who desires to be wise should trust in the Lord. His judgments are always true and righteous because He knows every detail of life—past, present and future. **Gold has a great value in man's eyes but the word of the Lord has the greatest value.** The word of the Lord is pure and proven. The book of Samuel reminds us that, "*As for* God, His way *is* perfect; The word of the Lord *is* proven; He *is* a shield to all who trust in Him" (2 Samuel 22:31).

Benefits of Trusting God

Here are some benefits of trusting in God based on Scripture:

1. **There is safety**

   "The fear of man brings a snare, But whoever trusts in the Lord shall be safe." (Proverbs 29:25)

2. **There is prosperity**

   He who is of a proud heart stirs up strife, But he who trusts in the Lord will be prospered. (Proverbs 28:25)

   He who trusts in his own heart is a fool, But whoever walks wisely will be delivered. (Proverbs 28:25–26)

3. **There is perfect peace**

   You will keep *him* in perfect peace, *Whose* mind *is* stayed *on You,* Because he trusts in You.
   Trust in the Lord forever, For in YAH, the Lord, *is* everlasting strength. (Isaiah 26:3–4)

4. **There is deliverance from the wicked**

   But the salvation of the righteous *is* from the Lord; *He is* their strength in the time of trouble. And the Lord shall help them and deliver them;

He shall deliver them from the wicked, And save them, Because they trust in Him. (Psalm 37:39–40)

5. There is blessedness

Oh, taste and see that the Lord *is* good; Blessed *is* the man *who* trusts in Him! (Psalm 34:8)

6. There is God's mercy

Many sorrows shall be to the wicked; But he who trusts in the Lord, mercy shall surround him. (Psalm 32:10)

7. You will be like Mount Zion

"Those who trust in the Lord, a*re* like Mount Zion,*Which* cannot be moved, *but* abides forever.

As the mountains surround Jerusalem, so the Lord surrounds His people, from this time forth and forever. (Psalm 125:1–2)

In this life, you and I can have safety, prosperity, perfect peace, and deliverance by trusting God. He loves us not only by words but by His action. Remember, "…God demonstrates His own love toward us, in that while we were still sinners, Christ died for us" (Romans 5:8). Lord Jesus sacrificing His life for us is the greatest sign of God's love. He endured great pain and He suffered much. He truly loves us. Father God does not change and He does not forget any promises He made.

I encourage you to put your trust in God above all because "*It is* better to trust in the Lord, than to put confidence in man. *It is* better to trust in the Lord, than to put confidence in princes" (Psalm 118:8–9). God is the sure foundation in this life. He created us and knows our greatest needs and desires. He has the greatest plan for your life. You can trust Him with your life. You can trust Him with your family and you can trust Him with your future. In your everyday life and daily decisions I advise you to "Trust in the Lord with all your heart, and lean not on your own understanding; in all your ways acknowledge Him, and He shall direct your paths" (Proverbs 3:5–6).

" He who heeds the word wisely will find good,
And whoever trusts in the Lord, happy is he." (Proverbs 16:20)

I challenge you to discover other KEYS or ways to please God. The goal of the Christian life is not to be rich or famous but to be like Christ in this sinful generation. I strongly believe that the keys presented here, if applied, will greatly help you in living in God's abundant life.

" Your word is a lamp to my feet and a light to my path."
(Psalm 119:105)

Life Lessons:

- *Trusting God above all will bring safety, prosperity and blessings in life.*

- *Our mind focused on God will bring the perfect peace we are looking for.*

Bible Study Discussion Questions:

1. As explained, how can we focus on God?

2. What are the benefits of trusting God?

3. Based on the story from Matthew 14:22–33, why did Peter start sinking? How can we apply this in our life?

4. Cite a verse on trusting God that you like and explain why?

5. In the Bible, do you remember a person who trusted in God and what was the result of his/her trust in God? In contrast, share about a person or people who do not trust in God and what happened?

6. In challenging times of our life, how can we keep our focus and trust in God despite difficulties or problems?

7. Based on the lesson and discussion, what can we apply in our daily life?

Part IV

Bonus

Topics

BONUS TOPIC 1

Why We Must Never Be Angry with God

I believe this is one of the most important parts of this book. Why? It is because many people are lost. Many people don't know how to deal with life's problems. I was once one of those who are angry with God. After learning the truth, I was delivered from the deception of our enemy.

The truth is God is our loving Father and Creator. He has given us everything we have. Consider the following:

Who gave you your life? It is God!

Who gives you air to breathe? It is God!

Who gave you your eyes to see? It is God!

Who gave you your arms to reach? It is God!

Who gave you your legs to walk? It is God!

For such good reasons, we must **never** be angry with God.

I've heard it said that, "If you have good health, you are wealthy." God loves mankind—All people, races and tribes, God loves them all. Satan made war against the angels of God but did not prevail (Revelation 12:7–8). I believe that because of Satan's great hatred for God, he wants to hurt God by hurting those who God loves.

In the story of the demoniac, which is told in Matthew chapter 17, it was a demon who caused the boy to suffer. The passage is shown below.

> [14] "And when they had come to the multitude, a man came to Him, kneeling down to Him and saying, [15] "Lord, have mercy on my son, for he is an epileptic and suffers severely; for he often falls into the fire and often into the water. [16] So I brought him to Your disciples, but they could not cure him."

[17] Then Jesus answered and said, "O faithless and perverse generation, how long shall I be with you? How long shall I bear with you? Bring him here to Me." [18] And Jesus rebuked the demon, and it came out of him; and the child was cured from that very hour." (Matthew 17:14–18)

Jesus, the Son of God, miraculously healed the boy. Instead of blaming God when we face difficulties, we must learn to do the opposite. We must learn to draw near to Him and recognize the enemy at work.

We have good examples in the Bible of those who learned to seek God and praise Him in the midst of their troubles. Job is one example. Remember that even though Job lost his children and his property, his first reaction to all the bad news was:

"Naked I came from my mother's womb,
And naked shall I return there.
The LORD gave, and the LORD has taken away;

Blessed be the name of the LORD." (Job 1:21)

Job praised the Lord despite a difficult situation. Then there was the story of when the apostles Paul and Silas were imprisoned in Acts 16. Let's see what happened to them and how they reacted towards God in the following passage:

[22] The crowd rose up together against them, and the chief magistrates tore their robes off them and proceeded to order them to be beaten with rods. [23] When they had struck them with many blows, they threw them into prison, commanding the jailer to guard them securely; [24] and he, having received such a command, threw them into the inner prison and fastened their feet in the stocks.

[25] But about midnight Paul and Silas were praying and singing hymns of praise to God,..." (Acts 16:22–25)

What an honorable attitude to have towards God who has given us everything we have! In a time of trouble, consider doing the opposite of pointing the finger at God. Praise Him. Pray to Him. Wait for Him.

In the time of king Jehoshaphat 3 armies set themselves against the people of Judah. Jehoshaphat said, "...Hear me, O Judah and you inhabitants of Jerusalem: Believe in the Lord your God, and you shall be established; believe His prophets, and you shall prosper" (2 Chronicles 20:20). When King Jehoshaphat sent out singers in front of the army, a miracle happened. Let's see what happened in verse 22:

> Now when they began to sing and to praise, the Lord set ambushes against the people of Ammon, Moab, and Mount Seir, who had come against Judah; and they were defeated. (2 Chronicles 20:22)

Important reasons to consider to avoid being angry with God

Aside from these 3 important examples, here are good reasons to help us remember why we must never be angry with God:

1. **God is good to us**

   God so loved man that He created a beautiful garden for man. He provided man with a helper. He provided everything they needed.

2. **God is love**

   God never intended to hurt Adam and Eve. Satan came with deceiving words to turn the heart of man and woman to disobey God. God never stopped loving Adam and Eve even though they sinned against Him. God provided clothing for them and He did not allow them to eat from the tree of life. Eating from the tree of life would bring man to everlasting separation from God (Genesis 3:24).

3. **God fulfilled His word**

God has a plan to rescue humanity (Genesis 3:15). This was fulfilled when Jesus gave His life as a ransom for many (Matthew 20:28). The Scriptures tell us that, "For as by one man's disobedience many were made sinners, so also by one Man's obedience many will be made righteous" (Romans 5:19).

4. All that God created was very good

The Bible says, "Then God saw everything that He had made, and indeed *it was* very good. So the evening and the morning were the sixth day (Genesis 1:31)."

Life Lessons:

- *Do not entertain the enemy when it comes to being angry with God*

- *When you catch yourself wanting to be angry with God, remember you should be doing the opposite*

BONUS TOPIC 2

Our Common Enemy:
Satan and His Demons

Sin originated in the heart of Satan who was once one of the chief angels in heaven. The Scripture says:

> "For you have said in your heart: 'I will ascend into heaven, I will exalt my throne above the stars of God; I will also sit on the mount of the congregation on the farthest sides of the north; I will ascend above the heights of the clouds, I will be like the Most High.'" (Isaiah 14:13–14)

Satan wanted to be like God Most High even though he was a created being. Satan's pride resulted in rebellion. It is written, "So the great dragon was cast out, that serpent of old, called the Devil and Satan, who deceives the whole world; he was cast to the earth, and his angels were cast out with him" (Revelation 12:9). Satan was thrown out of heaven along with his angels.

Other names for Satan are, "the devil" (Matthew 4:1); "the tempter" (1 Thessalonians 3:5); "Beelzebub" (Matthew 12:24); "the wicked one" (Matthew 13:19); "the ruler of this world" (John 12:31); "the god of this age" (2 Corinthians 4:4); "the prince of the power of the air" (Ephesians 2:2); "the great dragon, ...serpent of old" (Revelation 12:9); and "the father of lies" (John 8:44).

In Part I, we learned that the thief only comes to steal, kill and destroy (John 10:10). He has no good intention for mankind. Whoever agrees with Satan's deceptive words has sinned because there is no truth in him. Satan and his demons continue to deceive people around the world.

Genesis chapter 3 tells us of the fall of mankind. Satan, the "serpent of old" (Revelation 20:2), deceived Eve into eating the forbidden fruit. Eve gave the fruit to Adam and he ate. When Adam and Eve ate the forbidden fruit, sin first entered creation.

Satan is the same today. He will deceive us into believing that going after the lust of the flesh, lust of the eyes, and the pride of life will give us a better life. The lust of the flesh entered Eve when Eve saw that the tree was good for food. The lust of the eyes entered Eve when she considered that the tree "was pleasant to the eyes" so she would eat of it (Genesis 3:6). The pride of life entered Eve when she considered that the tree would make her wise.

The lust of the flesh, the lust of the eyes, and the pride of life are the great deception of our enemy. There's no truth in Satan. Many people around the world are deceived by the enemy. Many live to fulfill their lust for women or men. Many live to fulfill their lust for material things. Many live only to acquire things, or to become famous, rich and admired. It is a trap of the enemy. **Everlasting peace, love and joy come only from the Creator.**

It is not God's desire to see His creation suffer and die. Regarding the days of Noah, Scripture says:

> "Then the LORD saw that the wickedness of man was great in the earth, and that every intent of the thoughts of his heart was only evil continually. And the LORD was sorry that He had made man on the earth, and He was grieved in His heart." (Genesis 6:5–6)

The Lord experienced intense sorrow to see man's wickedness.

The origin of evil and sin will help us to answer the following questions: "Why do people suffer? Why is there famine? Why is there death? Why are there wars? And why is there so much violence in this world?"

Now we understand that the cause of all sin and evil is Satan, the deceiver and the father of lies who only comes to steal, kill and destroy. Understanding the origin of sin and evil will develop our love for God and His word and remind us of the need to be close to Him who is greater than the enemy.

Life Lessons:

- *Satan was once one of the chief angel of God*

- *Satan became a prideful fallen angel and has many rebellious angels under him*

- *The enemy's purpose is to steal, kill and destroy; to deceive everyone; and to promote the lust of the flesh, the lust of the eyes and the pride of life*

BONUS TOPIC 3

You Are More Than a Conqueror in Christ Jesus

This is my third bonus topic and encouragement to you. Romans 8:35–39 reads:

> 35 Who shall separate us from the love of Christ? Shall tribulation, or distress, or persecution, or famine, or nakedness, or peril, or sword? 36 As it is written:
>
> "For Your sake we are killed all day long;
>
> We are accounted as sheep for the slaughter."
>
> 37 Yet in all these things we are more than conquerors through Him who loved us. 38 For I am persuaded that neither death nor life, nor angels nor principalities nor powers, nor things present nor things to come, 39 nor height nor depth, nor any other created thing, shall be able to separate us from the love of God which is in Christ Jesus our Lord.

You are more than a conqueror through Christ Jesus. Scripture says that not a word will fail that the Lord God has spoken. **His words spoken are history written in advance**. His promises are true.

Psalm 33:9 reminds us of the power His words have. It says, "For He spoke, and it was done; He commanded, and it stood fast." God's words carry power in them, so when it says "you are more than a conqueror," you can have confidence that these words are true.

We are encouraged in the Bible not to cast away our confidence because there is a great reward for believers (Hebrews 10:35). I also want to encourage you of this. Do not be afraid of the different problems that may come in your life. God knows them already and He has a solution for every difficulty. Let us trust Him completely.

The New Living Translation of the Bible captures verse 37 of Romans 8 this way, "···No, despite all these things, **overwhelming victory is ours through Christ**, who loved us." The New American Standard Bible version similarly says, "…But in all these things **we overwhelmingly conquer through Him** who loved us" (Romans 8:37). Note, we don't just conquer, we conquer *overwhelmingly*!

Another important part of this message is that we conquer overwhelmingly *with Him*. Our assurance is *Him*. Why? His word is true. It is impossible for God to lie (Hebrews 6:18). Also, remember, He does not change (Malachi 3:6). We can be sure that *with Christ* we are more than conquerors because this is the way God put it in His unfailing Word. He would have left out the part that said "through Him" if Christ were not important to our overwhelming victory. But he made it clear that we are conquerors not in our own greatness, but *with Christ*. Jesus is at the center of the promise. And this makes sense because the Word says all authority in heaven and on Earth has been given to Him in Matthew 28:18.

Because of Jesus you are…

1. Empowered by His Spirit

2. Sealed by His Spirit

3. Able to do anything in His will

Life Lessons:

- *Overwhelming victory is promised for followers of Christ*

- *Victory can be achieved but not without **Him***

BONUS TOPIC 4

The Believer's Weapon:

Prayer and Fasting

In the generation we are living in, there are a lot of teachings about the grace of God. I have noticed that many believers are not regularly fasting. I believe one reason for that is the excessive teaching on the grace of God. Lord God the Holy Spirit revealed to me what is lacking in my life and it concerned the area of fasting.

In Matthew chapter 6, there are 3 commandments: when you give…when you pray…and when you fast. The area of fasting is the hardest to follow. Lord Jesus said, "…But the days will come when the bridegroom will be taken away from them, and they will fast" (Matthew 9:15). These days are the days Lord Jesus is commanding His church to fast. Fasting must be part of life as a follower of Jesus.

Let us read a wonderful story on the importance of fasting.

A boy is healed

[14] And when they had come to the multitude, a man came to Him, kneeling down to Him and saying, [15] "Lord, have mercy on my son, for he is an epileptic[a] and suffers severely; for he often falls into the fire and often into the water. [16] So I brought him to Your disciples, but they could not cure him."

[17] Then Jesus answered and said, "O faithless and perverse generation, how long shall I be with you? How long shall I bear with you? Bring him here to Me." [18] And Jesus rebuked the demon, and it came out of him; and the child was cured from that very hour.

[19] Then the disciples came to Jesus privately and said,

"Why could we not cast it out?"

[20] So Jesus said to them, "Because of your unbelief;[b] for assuredly, I say to you, if you have faith as a mustard seed, you will say to this mountain, 'Move from here to there,' and it will move; and nothing will be impossible for you. [21] *However, this kind does not go out except by prayer and fasting."* (Matthew 17:14–21)

All of the disciples encountered a kind of demon that could only be cast out by "prayer and fasting." Lord Jesus revealed a powerful truth on the importance of fasting. **I can say with all my heart that prayer and fasting is a weapon available to every believer.** Every believer must know how to use this God-given command to fast to live a victorious life.

Is there some difficulty when a person begins to fast? Yes! There can be pain, headaches, dizziness and, especially, hunger. God commanded every believer to "present your bodies a living sacrifice, holy, acceptable to God, which is your reasonable service" (Romans 12:1).

Apostle Paul fasted often (2 Corinthians 11:27). On one occasion, Lord Jesus was asked by His disciples to eat but He replied, "My food is to do the will of Him who sent Me, and to finish His work" (John 4:34). Lord Jesus is our example of how to live our life on Earth. The Bible says, "Man shall not live by bread alone, but by every word that proceeds from the mouth of God" (Matthew 4:4).

I know a brother in the Lord who fasted and prayed for 21 days and after that, a miracle happened in his life. His wife decided to come back home after a difficult time of being separated. He paid the price of enduring some pain and hunger in prayer and fasting, and it resulted in him, his wife and his children being reunited. I believe that the demon harassing them was cast out of their family. He rejoiced greatly. He glorified God, giving thanks to Him for bringing back his wife.

As a follower of Jesus, if you are not fasting I encourage you to obey the Lord in this area of your life. (It can be the Daniel Fast, a water fast, or a full fast.) This is especially important in difficult or challenging times of our life here on Earth. Satan and his demons are here on earth only to kill, steal and destroy us.

We have to ask the Holy Spirit to guide and lead us on the seasons of prayer and fasting. He is the Spirit of truth and there's no unrighteousness in Him. His way is the perfect way for us. If we are willing to obey, God the Holy Spirit can enable us by His grace to fast for many days and accomplish His will for our lives.

Life Lessons:

- *Fasting must be part of life as a follower of Jesus*

- *There are some kinds of problems in our lives that may only be solved through prayer and fasting*

- *The Holy Spirit can enable us even when fasting seems difficult*

BONUS TOPIC 5

The Truth About Denying One's Self

The sin of Adam & Eve has resulted in us having a sinful nature. The sinful nature is the seed of Satan to man. As believers, we have a new nature in Christ Jesus but we have a daily responsibility to deny ourselves. Lord Jesus said, "If anyone desires to come after Me, let him deny himself, and take up his cross, and follow Me" (Matthew 16:24).

Why does the self-will have to be denied? As disciples of Jesus, we are servants of the Lord. Self has to be denied so that we don't do what we want to do but only the will of the Father. Lord Jesus said, "I can of Myself do nothing. As I hear, I judge; and My judgment is righteous, because I do not seek My own will but the will of the Father who sent Me" (John 5:30). The self-will is a hindrance to the work of God. The sinful nature of man has several names in the Bible which are the following:

1. The body of sin (Romans 6:6)

2. The body of death (Romans 7:24)

3. The flesh (Romans 7:18). Nothing good dwells and it cannot please God (Romans 8:8)

4. The old man (Romans 6:6)

This sinful nature, the body of sin, the body of death, the flesh, or the old man walks CONTRARY to the Spirit (Galations 5:17). As the temple of God (1 Corinthians 3:16), below are God's commands for our body:

1. Make it walk according to the Spirit (Romans 8:1)

2. Make it a living sacrifice (Romans 12:1)

3. Bring it under control (1 Corinthians 9:27)

4. Make it fit as the temple of the Holy Spirit (1 Corinthians 3:17)

5. Do not let sin reign (Romans 6:12)

6. Put to death its deeds (Romans 8:13)

7. Keep it from sexual immorality (1 Corinthians 6:13)

8. Glorify God in it (1 Corinthians 6:20)

9. Discipline it (1 Corinthians 9:27)

10. Make no provision for the flesh (Romans 13:14)

By the grace and mercy of God, we can live victoriously in this life even though we live in this body of death. Apostle Paul mentioned, "O wretched man that I am! Who will deliver me from this body of death?" (Romans 7:24). God the Holy Spirit is able to help us overcome this body of sin as God's word says, "I can do all things through Christ who strengthens me (Philippians 4:13). "…May your whole spirit, soul, and body be preserved blameless at the coming of our Lord Jesus Christ" (1Thessalonians 5:23).

Life Lessons:

- *There is a sinful nature in man*

- *As believers, we have a daily responsibility to deny ourselves*

Part V

Conclusion with a

Miracle Story

$\mathcal{I}$named this book "Finding Abundant Life in Jesus" because I believe that true success or victory in life is found only in entrusting our lives in the hands of the One who loves us and died for us—the "King of kings and Lord of lords (Revelation 19:16)," Jesus Christ.

God has good things to say about the one who follows Him. No matter what people say or do, God's word remains true and He who promised is faithful. It is my prayer that you will be committed to obeying and loving God above all, no matter how challenging your circumstances are in life.

The main reason I wrote this book is to encourage you that there is hope in life through Jesus Christ. You can find abundant life by abiding in Jesus. He loves you and He is willing to help you. He wants to be involved in all areas of your life. He wants to give you the best because He has a perfect plan for your life.

Psalm 27:10 says, "When my father and my mother forsake me, then the Lord will take care of me." At a time in my life when I felt forsaken by my parents, the Lord came and turned my situation around.

Our God is a God of miracles

Upon writing this book, I'm now 40 years old. I am married with 2 children and we are living in Canada. There was another miracle that happened last year in April of 2015. I asked God to surprise me on my birthday. Then I received a message from Brother Rohan, who is in charge of our church website. He told me that someone from Batangas, Philippines wanted to get hold of me. I called and it was my cousin from my father's side who was trying to reach me. She said that my father wanted to see me. She gave me my father's phone number. So I started to communicate with him after 39 years.

Reunited with my father after 39 Years

My father sent me a text message saying, "The Lord Jesus answered your prayers." He said he was thinking of me all of these years and realized that I was indeed one of his sons. He requested that I come home to the Philippines and meet him and called me his son for the first time. After sharing this with my wife and daughter, I said "yes" to my father. I learned that his 74th birthday would be in August of 2015.

A picture with my father on his 74th birthday at his favorite Philippine restaurant

We did catch up with each other. I felt the love he has for me; I know it was the working of the Lord. He listened to every story I had to tell him. He shared why he left us and in my heart, I had already forgiven him. I shared about the Lord Jesus and we prayed many times. On my last days in the Philippines, we met and hugged each other. Until today, we have kept on communicating. I have discovered the goodness in the heart of my earthly father.

Obeying God's still small voice

A friend asked me why my father changed his mind. My answer was from Deuteronomy 28:1–2, "If you diligently obey the voice of the Lord your God and keep His commandments…then the blessings of God shall come upon you and overtake you."

I have learned the importance of following God's still small voice. **I consider God's still small voice as a command by the heavenly Father and Lord Jesus** (John 16:13–15).

The Holy Spirit =

Spirit of His Son (Galatians 4:6) =

Spirit of your Father (Matthew 10:20)

Lord Jesus said, "I will not leave you orphans; I will come to you"(John 14:18) and "…I am with you always, even to the end of the age" (Matthew 28:20). The Bible says that "…God has revealed *them* to us through His Spirit. For the Spirit searches all things, yes, the deep things of God. For what man knows the things of a man except the spirit of the man which is in him? Even so no one knows the things of God except the Spirit of God. Now we have received, not the spirit of the world, but the Spirit who is from God, that we might know the things that have been freely given to us by God" (1 Corinthians 2:10–12). In 2011, I heard the still small voice of God after I worshipped Him, asking Him for His direction for my life. He spoke words to my heart and at the end of His words came supernatural joy. I understood that it was God, because in the presence of God there is fullness of joy and I am the temple of the Holy Spirit (Psalm 16:11, 1 Corinthians 3:16). I also understood that His sheep hear His voice. Therefore, I prayerfully dropped everything I was doing and followed His voice. I know that He declares the end from the beginning and has all power in all things to fulfill every promise He has spoken to me. I believed the scripture that says not a word will fail which the Lord God has spoken (Joshua 21:45).

In the beginning, I encountered a lot of difficulty in following God's direction, but now, I have no plans but His plans for my life. Psalm 31:15 says, "My times are in Your hand," and so I have given my life to Him. He gives me step-by-step direction as I continuously seek Him. I can testify God provides everything we need. He makes a way where there seems no way and He is faithful and true. He is a Good Shepherd. Great is His faithfulness.

Our God is amazing. He is awesome, a wonderful Master and a faithful God. God touched the heart of my father. Twenty-one years passed between the time I first met him, when I went searching for him at the age of 18 years old (See Part II), and the time of our reunion.

As a Christian minister, I encourage you to follow the 7 KEYS with all of your heart, which are (1) Believe God Above All (2) Have Faith in God (3) Love God Above All and Unconditionally (4) Obey God Above All (5) Fear God Above All (6) Keep God's Commandments (7) Focus on God and Trust in Him. I guarantee you that you will be rewarded for obeying God's word. Problems will come but God is able to help and strengthen us to overcome them all. He is faithful to fulfill His written word (the Bible) and His still small voice (John 10:16). He does not lie and does not change. He has all power to make it happen.

God is the "Great Rewarder" in this life and the coming eternal life. A faithful man or woman shall abound in blessings. Our obedience, love, faith and trust in God will surely harvest many blessings. Choose to serve Him only and your life will never be the same.

Special Thanks

To **Father God, Lord Jesus and Lord Holy Spirit** for granting me wisdom, understanding and knowledge to complete this book. I am very thankful to God for His gift of life and His provision for our every need. God is my strength, wisdom, rock, fortress, deliverer, shield, stronghold, hope, peace, greatest encourager and helper. He is my everything.

To my supportive wife Jennifer Castillo, who reviewed this book, who loves me unconditionally and always prays for me. My lovely wife took the beautiful photos included in this book.

To all those who reviewed and edited this manuscript: my daughter Angel Castillo, my sister Ruth Castillo, Zorena and Ramesh Mahendar, and Cherry and Anita Thomas.

Special acknowledgements to Dr. Paul Magnus and his wife, Sis Jane, for their continued support and prayers, and Dr. Randy Neilson for his endorsement, support and prayers.

To Aisha Hammah for editing and publishing this book, who went the extra mile in completing this project.

To our loving and supportive BCF Church family and other church family and friends.

To our family, relatives and friends who support and pray for us.

To all who will use, promote and distribute this book for the advancement of God's kingdom.

A Tribute

I want to give tribute to <u>Brother Cecil Owen Staple</u> who went home to be with Lord Jesus on March 28, 2016. He was a faithful brother in the Lord. He has touched my life and others because of his love and dedication to the Lord. He prayed for this book.

To purchase books visit...

www.wtlipublishing.com

Or for more information you can send an email to one of the following addresses...

ah@wtlipublishing.com

You can contact the author at the email addresses below:

ruelhcastillo@yahoo.ca

ruelhcastillo0529@gmail.com

castillojennifer22@yahoo.ca